FRED T. PERRIS IN DESERET

FRED T. PERRIS IN DESERET

NEIL JENSEN

authorHOUSE®

AuthorHouse™
1663 Liberty Drive
Bloomington, IN 47403
www.authorhouse.com
Phone: 1-800-839-8640

Published by AuthorHouse   10/08/2012

ISBN: 978-1-4772-4831-7 (sc)
ISBN: 978-1-4772-5592-6 (e)

Library of Congress Control Number: 2012914103

This book is printed on acid-free paper.

Cover design by Teddi Jensen
www.teddijensen.com

Fred T. Perris at 75

Fred T. Perris surrounded by his survey crew, circa 1882

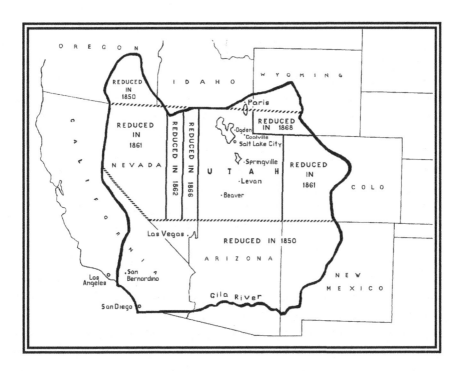

The proposed State of Deseret, 1849

The Book of Mormon, the foundation document of the Mormon movement, tells the story of ancient peoples migrating to America. *"And they did also carry with them deseret, which, by interpretation, is a honey bee."* (Ether 2:3) From this single, obscure reference, the State of Utah incorporates a beehive into its state flag. The state motto is "Industry." Their ideal model of society is the beehive, where everyone is busy. The Mormons wanted their state to be called Deseret, but Congress named it Utah, and changed its boundaries frequently.

LIST OF ILLUSTRATIONS

The illustrations, copies of copies, come from a variety of publications, that themselves were copies, often failing to identify their sources. All of which are long since in the public domain. Hopefully additional research will identify the ownership of the originals, such that in any future printings, proper credit may be given.

PREFACE

I grew up in Salt Lake City in a devout Mormon family. Oddly enough, I was raised without the presence of grandparents, which resulted in my lifelong feeling that I was cut off from a personal identification with history. Perhaps this was the origin of my incessant hunger for the subject. I was imbued with that particular way of thinking and viewing the cosmos that makes the Mormons unique, at least in their own eyes. At the knees of my parents I heard stories of the many miraculous occurrences, miracles, no less, that my ancestry had experienced, as they struggled across the plains to settle Utah, and to build the Church. These were always faith promoting stories with the promise that if I lived as faithful a life as they did, miraculous interventions would come my way as well. They never did, but that's another story. The point of all this is that, despite all the emphasis Mormons put upon genealogy, I knew very little, practically nothing, about my forebears, how they lived, how they felt about issues, or even how they earned a living.

From time to time my father would mention his great uncle, Fred, whose claim to fame was that he ran a clothing store over on West Temple Street, and who built a railroad in Southern California. He said his uncle, for whom he was named, was a famous man, but I always discounted that as just an oblique way of his to try to put a little praise to his own name. How little I knew. How little he knew.

A couple of years ago he asked me to create a short play for an upcoming family reunion, suggesting a story about his grandmother, Fanny Jane Perris, Fred's sister, on her wedding day. That's got to be good family reunion fare. Church records showed it was four days after Christmas, 1857, in, of all places, Las Vegas! She was fifteen at the time. He was twenty one—what kind of scandal was this? I had learned the first law of genealogy. Don't look, if you can't stand to find out things you didn't want to know. And the first plot complication of the play was, how would I present that kind of subject matter to an audience composed primarily of Mormons and their children? My father suggested I not stress that part of her story, but without it, there wasn't much story left.—except the adventures of her brother Fred, who's name kept popping up everywhere I looked in California history.

It is not entirely true there wasn't a faith promoting story to be found about Grandma Fanny Jane. After all, it turns out, they were in Las Vegas, on their way from San Bernardino to Utah, to answer the call of the Lord—Brigham Young, anyway, who had called them to the mountaintops in preparation for the 2nd Coming. But far more interesting, to me anyway, was the discovery of her brother Fred, and his many achievements in his later life, after he returned to California. It's all well documented. Finding out what he did in Utah was not as easy. His name and legacy there seem to have been forgotten with an amazing intensity, just

Fred T. Perris

erased from the public consciousness. Even the newspaper he helped to found has not a single mention of his name in their library. Researching this material has been like a detective story, as the facts of his life were gradually and painstakingly uncovered.

There are many people to thank for their assistance, including casual strangers in Coalville and Idaho who talked about the early days of their communities. Lezann Pilgrim, in the Marriott Library at the University of Utah, was particularly helpful, and the unsung heroine, a graduate student, who cataloged all the Hampton C. Godbe papers deserves mention. They helped locate two never before published letters from Fred Perris.

My thanks also to my daughter Teddi, and to my wife Martha, for their countless proof readings and thoughtful critiques. Without them both this project would never have come this far.

Neil Jensen,
Mountain View, California
1995

PREFACE
to the 2nd Edition

In the years since I first put this little book together, my interest in Uncle Fred has continued. Further research about his life and times naturally turned up additional information which required some clarification and correction of previous conjectures. Research certainly isn't like it used to be. Formerly I traveled great distances, and spent days in obscure libraries searching for scraps of information in dusty old volumes. At one time I had in my possession a first edition copy of one volume of the three volume set, Whitney's History of Utah. It contained an account of the Morrisite War. I gave the book away, to restore the set; and then I kicked myself for losing the vital facts about the affair. In a moment of despair I Googled "Morrisite War," and there: Wikipedia had an article on the whole business, with a reference to the very book I lost. Furthermore, if I wanted to buy that reference book, a reprint was available at Amazon. Yes, research ain't what it used to be.

N J 2012

Dedicated to my father, Perris Jensen

Frederick Thomas Perris was a civil engineer who surveyed and built railroad lines in Southern California. There are a number of landmarks named for him, including the City of Perris, in Riverside County; as well as the Perris Hill Municipal Park in San Bernardino, on land he donated to the city. In 1857 he left California and was away until 1874. Most of that time he spent in Utah. After returning to California he didn't talk a great deal about it, as though hoping to put that chapter of his life behind him. Nevertheless, he left an achievement there that is no less significant than any of his works in Southern California; but of a completely different nature. The legacy he left in Utah is an institution that was, and still is, second only to the dominating LDS Church (Mormon) in its influence and political persuasion, namely, *The Salt Lake Tribune*. He was one of the founders of the paper. This is the only major independent newspaper in the state, and has been since 1870. The word "independent" means not owned and operated by the Mormon Church.[1] It was born on the wild frontier, not as a business enterprise to sell newsprint, and report the events of the day, but as a strident, political weapon in an ideological war for control of the Territory. He and the newspaper rallied the liberal cause, and forced two-party politics into a one-party town going head to head with the indomitable Brigham Young and his powerful politico/ecclesiastical hierarchy. For a period of two years Fred Perris was literally the lone voice of opposition, the only one in a seemingly failed movement, who dared to put his name on the masthead of the combative publication.[2] While he is remembered in Southern California as a competent and dedicated civil engineer, the Utah episode of his life reveals an entirely different side of this extraordinary and talented man.

He first saw California in 1849, as a boy of twelve, landing briefly in San Francisco with his parents and two younger sisters at the height of the gold rush.[3] At first glance, one is tempted to think his father was attracted by the gold, but closer examination finds that isn't quite accurate. His father, Thomas Perris, was a successful broker on the docks in Gloucester, England (GLAH-stir, rhymes with CLAW-stir). He was a family man, with a wife, four children, and social prestige, quite unlikely to be tempted by rumors of free gold somewhere halfway around the world. Furthermore, gold seekers were men traveling alone, not with children; certainly not with a baby still in its mother's arms! A far more compelling reason for the entire family to have up and left their ancestral homeland was the plague that swept across Gloucestershire in 1849. Tom Perris knew something about that. His brother John was a veternarian living in the country. Two of John's children died one night of a mysterious ailment, and six weeks later a third child was dead.[4] Tom Perris was quick to see a plague, even though the officials were slow to admit it. If word got out that there was a plague, the port would close. Ships would simply refuse to dock, and brokers, such as himself, would be out of business. Scientists later categorized this plague as typhoid. There were several theories as to its cause. Fred's mother, Hannah Rebecca

Gloucester

The British Isles

Spiller Perris, was undoubtedly familiar with the all the Biblical references to the subject of plagues.

Tom Perris liquidated his assets. They packed up the children and set out for Australia, probably from the port at Southampton. The British Crown was offering generous incentives to immigrants, particularly British subjects. to settle there. Steamships plied the oceans. Travel was much safer and more comfortable than the old fashioned sailing ships, which were quickly becoming obsolete. For some reason, however, child mortality remained high. Little Ida Perris, age 3, their third child, died at sea, before they even completed the first leg of their trip, to Chagres. From there it was a four day trip overland to Panama City on the Pacific coast, reducing the travel time to Australia from months to a matter of weeks. They found however, upon arriving in Panama, that this old Spanish colonial town, with facilities for a few hundred travelers at any one time, was packed with some three thousand people all vying to get to San Francisco[5]—which apparently was the only place that ships were going anyway.

A kind of impromptu stock market had sprung into operation, trading in ship passage future, with bid and asked prices being posted hourly at a travel agent's office, rising and falling on rumors and the likelihood of such and such a ship, due to make a port call, actually doing so.

2

Tom Perris was familiar with this game. Eventually he booked passage for his family as far as San Francisco, where the sailors promptly jumped ship, and ran off to go gather up some free gold.

That is how Fred Perris at age 12 came to be in San Francisco in 1849.[6] In due course, the sailors returned from the gold fields, most likely satisfied that life aboard a luxury steamship was preferable to digging sand in a cold river, and sleeping on the ground. The ship proceeded on her way to Australia. Tom Perris did well financially in the time he was there. After a short stay in Sydney, the family moved to upscale Melbourne where the climate and lifestyle were more reminiscent of England. He opened a furniture store there, and profited greatly from the economic bump that came when gold was also discovered near Melbourne. Fred entered an apprenticeship with an architect/mechanic, where he got his first exposure to math and drafting. He did not complete the program.

His mother, Hannah, was a woman of small stature, but bursting with energy.[7] She was twelve years younger than her husband, and probably not included in his all-male society. She was waited upon hand and foot. The children were well cared for. All her material needs were met, leaving her with nothing to do. Then two LDS missionaries knocked on her door and things changed. Their message was simple. Tom's response was also simple, an ultimatum. He said she could have that obscure church, located somewhere out in the wilds of Western America; or she could have his money and growing prestige in an upstanding community, but not both;[8] whereupon she filed for divorce, packed up her daughters, took her son back from his apprenticeship, joined a traveling company of Mormon converts and sailed for America.

Mormon missionaries have always sought out the cheapest transportation, mainly because they have so little money. In this case they booked passage on an old sailing ship, retired from the Royal British Navy after transporting convicts to Australia.

She set sail from Melbourne on April 6, 1853.[9] The time at sea for these aging vessels could be 90 days or more from Melbourne to America, meaning it was the first part of July when the ship dropped anchor in San Pedro Harbor, south of Los Angeles. It wasn't a pleasant voyage.

Collins Street, Melbourne, 1851

Hannah Rebecca Spiller Perris Stewart
1820 - 1901

3

Fred's mother, Hannah, vowed never to make another ocean voyage, a vow she ultimately could not keep. Instead of proceeding on to Salt Lake City with the main body of the traveling company, Hannah and her three children joined the new Mormon settlement at Rancho San Bernardino, that had only been established two years earlier. This had to have been something of a major culture shock for the woman and her children, accustomed as they were to the luxuries of the Victorian merchant class, taking up residence in a commune called Fort San Bernardino.

Some history of San Bernardino is in order: In 1846 after the Mormons had abandoned their settlement in western Illinois, and begun their exodus to Utah, the US Army set about mobilizing a major campaign against Mexico, and recruited five hundred Mormon volunteers.[10] Colonel Thomas L. Kane, the recruiting officer agreed to paying the recruits in advance, the money going to Brigham Young, the Mormon leader, to defray the costs of moving the families of those men westward to the new Zion. This contingent of volunteers, known as the Mormon Battalion, marched from Fort Leavenworth, to Santa Fe, and then on to San Diego looking for a Mexican force to engage. They never found an enemy; but they found a very balmy climate in Southern California, and lots of cheap real estate.

Isaac Williams owned Rancho Chino, having married into the family that had owned the original Mexican land grant. He told the Mormon soldiers he was fed up with California and the constant struggle to survive on semi-arid land. He was in ill health, and ready to sell his entire spread to the first reasonable offer.[11]

The troops of the Mormon Battalion mustered out of the military in San Diego, and found their way to Salt Lake City where their families and the main body of the Church had settled; and the land and the climate gave new meaning to the word arid. Some of them started promoting the idea of another Mormon

San Bernardino, 1852

4

settlement in Southern California, a sort of southern outpost for an independent Mormon empire that seemed to be on everyone's minds at the time.

Brigham Young, of course, had other ideas, and sent a lobbyist to Washington to petition Congress for admission into the Union. He allowed the idea of a southern colony to go forward, thinking a dozen or so people might be interested; but was taken aback when 150 families, some 450 people, signed up to form a traveling company.[12]

The year was 1851. After twelve arduous weeks on the road, actually creating the road as they went (now Interstate Freeway 15), they arrived in an emaciated condition.[13] Isaac Williams was alarmed. He thought he had agreed to sell Rancho Chino to two or three families; but 450 was out of the question. There was no way the land could support that many people. He wouldn't sell. This must have left the Mormons feeling rather stranded, and perhaps a little desperate. Nearby, Rancho San Bernardino was essentially vacant. There had been previous occupation; but when Jose Lugo and his wife died, their descendants found they preferred the milder climate of Los Angeles, and the rancho fell into disuse. The vineyard died, and the fruit orchard also.

The Mormons set up camp, in a word, "squatted," as there was no one to oppose them. They immediately planted 20 acres of grain,[14] and then they sought out the owners of the land to arrange a purchase. The Lugo heirs were probably glad to unload the place. The compromise selling price was $77,500, which the leaders of the

expedition, Amasa Lyman and Charles C. Rich, borrowed on a personal note at 3% interest per month.[15] Ouch!

What they got for their purchase was a five room adobe hacienda, in serious need of repair, plus a couple of adobe sheds which Franciscan monks had built in the previous century; and all the land, not quite the whole valley, but certainly enough to build their dream community. They thought they had purchased 80,000 acres, about a dollar an acre. The title was in Spanish and none of the Mormons was especially fluent in that language. The Lugos didn't know where the property line was. Nobody ever worried about it before. The title defined the Northern boundary as "El Faldo de Sierras," or the brow of the mountains—wherever that might be.[16]

It took a federal commission a year to untangle the vagueness of this, and all the Mexican land grants in California, which the United States had agreed to honor in the treaty that ended the war with Mexico. Their ruling defined Rancho San Bernardino as eight square leagues, or about 36,000 acres, giving the owners, Lyman and Rich, the option of staking out exactly where the property line would be.

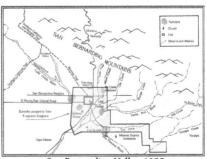

San Bernardino Valley, 1855

The Los Angeles Times wrote an editorial welcoming the industrious Mormons to the neighborhood, and looked forward to their contribution to the general welfare; but the sudden influx of nearly five hundred settlers must have been troublesome to the few bands of native peoples subsisting, in the area as hunter-gatherers. The exact nature of the conflict between the two cultures is hard to determine. Most of the Mormon settlers were from parts of the US where violent conflicts between natives and settlers were in very recent history; but there is no comparison between the threat of the highly organized Iroquois Nation in the Northeast and the primitive "diggers" of the Sonora Desert who had been decimated by a smallpox epidemic two decades earlier. It is likely that they did eat some of the Mormon livestock. That's what people do when they are hungry.

The Mormon response was to build a fortress, some 300 by 700 feet, with cabins or cubicles facing inward, to provide each family with a space, however cramped. Here they stayed for nearly two years, until a vigilante group of settlers came together from as far away as Ventura, Santa Barbara and San Diego counties, and took to the field. Nothing was ever recorded of this ad hoc militia's activities; but thereafter the fear of "Indian" attacks receded. Individual Mormons became restive, and anxious to expand outside of

the compound. By the summer of 1853 they began to feel secure enough to start putting up cabins and barns outside the fort walls. Their harvests were successful. Their herds were increasing. They replanted the orchard and the vineyard. They were an industrious people and their efforts paid off.

Lyman and Rich, the leaders of the enterprise, if nothing else, were practical. They quickly realized that private ownership of assets, i.e. real estate, not only stimulates civic pride and participation, which communal living can never do without a strict dictator; but it also distributes the debt load. If just the two of them own all the land, and missed a single mortgage payment, the whole enterprise fails; whereas if 150 or more people own the land, any one of them can fail; but the community persists. That was more important to Lyman and Rich than amassing huge wealth for themselves at the expense of others.

To subdivide the land they needed a surveyor; and hired Henry Sherwood, who had recently surveyed and laid out Salt Lake City, to come to Southern California and do the same thing. He arrived around the end of June with his family and survey crew.

In the meantime, the problem of over-crowding in the fort was exacerbated by the arrival of three dozen emigrants

Fort San Bernardino 1853

from Australia, including a pert and attractive divorcee, Hannah Perris, who looked far too young to have a sixteen year old son. Her marital status was in danger from the moment she entered the compound, and indeed, within a year she married Mathew Stewart, a stalwart member of the faith, from Ohio.

When the bishop met Fred, and learned of his apprenticeship in Melbourne, incomplete though it was, he was immediately put to work on Henry Sherwood's survey crew as a chain boy. He was quick to learn, and soon mastered all the skills and steps needed to make an accurate survey. He proved to be very thorough in his work, and

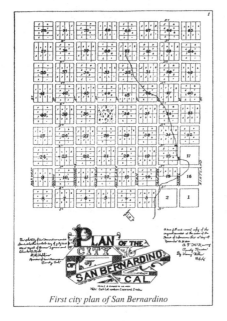

First city plan of San Bernardino

kept daily notes on pads of yellow paper, of every feature, be it rock formation, gully or streambed, even though that probably wasn't required for the job.[17] When the field work was completed he moved right into the office, sat down

at a drafting board, and began drawing maps and city plans.

When Fred finished the city plan, they offered parcels of land for sale. On the first day of the offer Fred and his mother each purchased a lot for $100.[18]

The community prospered. Everyone was employed. They built an impossibly steep road into the mountains, and brought down timber, cut it into lumber, and sold it, as well as farm produce to the endless market in Los Angeles. Lyman and Rich remained heavily in debt.

They set about the task of organizing a civil government, as distinct from Los Angeles County, by getting a measure on the ballot, which, of course all the Mormons voted for, thus creating the County of San Bernardino out of the eastern part of Los Angeles County. Fred Perris went to work in the new County Recorder's office as a clerk.

The official county records in the archives, preprinted forms filled out in Fred's legible handwriting, reveal the origin of San Bernardino's contemptible nickname. He wrote out hundreds of land titles; and in the blank space for county he abbreviated it to San Brdo.

And some wag, must have voiced his insolent objection by asking: "Hey, what's the name of this here place, San BerDOO?"

And the name stuck.

Fred was just trying to save time. Diligence was part of his nature. At some point he also worked on a mineral survey crew for the state government.[19]

Homes and commercial buildings suddenly started going up all over town. They thanked God for their bounteous harvest, and had people join the church, though membership was not a requirement to live in the growing town. But alas, there was trouble in paradise.

There always is. This Mormon colony, going through the curious transition from a communal society to free enterprise, always letting the practical trump the religious or doctrinal purity, was, technically speaking, an economic success. Whether or not that is the ultimate measure of all things is another matter. The original 450 settlers in 1851 grew to about 1,000 by 1857, of varying degrees of commitment to the cause. The enterprise remained deeply in debt, but their living standards had improved considerably in the six years they had lived here.

To their chagrin, the reality of the San Bernardino colony fell short of the ideal. Those who fell short of total obedience to the leaders were held to be the ones responsible. All too soon there came to be two kinds of people, the saints and the sinners, the good guys, and the not so good guys; and the gulf between them widened over time. The first overt friction came on July 4, 1854 when a scuffle broke out at the town picnic over how appropriate the patriotic speaker was, who was simply reading an article from last year's *Deseret News*.[20]

That's what happens in a perfect society, where everyone's basic needs are being met. Guys run out of things to fight about, and are reduced to finding trivial issues to fulfill some primitive or perhaps hormonal need to contend in combat, test their strength against others. Furthermore, there were reports of drunkenness and disorderly behavior, obviously rowdies from out of town. Settling your differences with

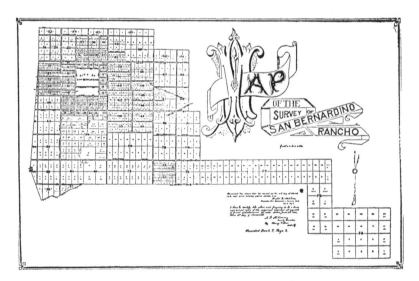

a fight was all the vogue in these days leading up to the Civil War.

The following year, hoping to prevent a repeat of last year's senseless violence, they held two separate Fourth of July

www.ci.san-bernardino.ca.us/about/history/4th_of_july.asp

celebrations, which turned the two events into a patriotism contest.[21] Who had the biggest flag, or which side had the spiffiest uniforms for the marching band, or the loudest fireworks? The anti-Mormon crowd won that contest with an old cannon used in the Mexican War that someone had dragged over

from Los Angeles for the occasion. By the next year (1856) the two factions were separated by that cannon, aimed to fire upon any Mormon who might approach.

Jerome Benson (no relation to Ezra Taft Benson) joined the San Bernardino colony in 1854, but very soon fell into disfavor with the Church leadership. They expected every member of the congregation to buy a piece of property to help distribute the financial obligation of the enterprise. Benson declined. He crossed the river, staked out a property and claimed it as homestead without buying anything from anybody. When Lyman and Rich sought a court order to evict him, he argued that the Mormon survey was inaccurate, and the Mormon judge should not even hear this case. When the Mormon sheriff came to serve an eviction notice, Benson's friends had rallied to the cause, fortified his home, and prepared for mortal combat, mounting the cannon in the wall. It came to be known as Fort Benson.

Fort Benson, 1856

9

Somebody made a pencil sketch of it. The anti-Mormons held their Fourth of July celebration there in 1856. It stood in defiance to the authorities for over a year, but in the end the conflict was resolved peacefully.

Rank and file Mormons were outraged. The economy was expanding, but the quality of life was declining. They had worked so hard, sacrificed so much, endured so many privations to build a new and perfect society according to God's true law, and what came from all that effort was this terrible dystopia. The strife was so intense that no decent person would even want to live there, let alone raise their children in such a negative environment. Many blamed their economic success as the cause of the spiritual and social failure.

To make matters worse, they couldn't even agree on whom to blame, or what to do; but something had to change.

Meanwhile, in faraway Washington, where conspiracies are a way of life, political events were about to boil over. The new president, James Buchanan, taking office in the spring of 1857, inherited a difficult problem from the previous administration, in the form of the contentious Territory of Utah. It lay astride the main roadway between the eastern states and California. Thousands of people passed along that trail every year; yet those travelers felt the territory was lawless and essentially out of control. Three federal judges appointed in Utah, shortly after it was organized as a territory, got on badly with the community, and left after only three months, taking the gold with them that they had brought to set up the

federal offices in town. Others came and fared no better, leaving for fear of their lives.[22] One federal judge who came to replace a runaway judge, retired to bed one night, and was found dead in his room the next morning, propelling the rumor that he had been poisoned. Brigham Young had a fearsome band of destroying angels; or at least they had a fearsome reputation.[23]

Over a seven year period a dozen or so officials had come and gone in trying to keep just three federal judges on the bench. The Territorial Legislature, in trying to prove that no federal government was needed in these parts, passed legislation to empower local courts to handle cases that would otherwise be taken to a Federal Court.

There were repeated claims that the Mormons were in a state of rebellion, refusing to recognize the sovereignty of the United States, and planning the establishment of an independent state. The governor of the territory was Brigham Young, who was also the leader of the Mormon Church, an uncomfortable situation whenever the topic of separation of church and state came up. His term of office as territorial governor had expired three years prior; but, for whatever reason, the previous president had neither extended Brigham Young's term, nor appointed another governor to replace him.

So, Buchanan did what needed to be done, and appointed Alfred Cumming from Georgia, who had never seen the territory, to be governor. To see that he was properly installed as governor, Buchanan sent along a military escort of some twenty five hundred troops;

and as if that weren't enough, he sent another thousand the next year. That's a lot of soldiers, considering the fact that the entire army was only eight thousand men. Their task was to "put down the rebellion" in Utah.

Were the Mormons really in a state of rebellion in 1857-'58? Evidence can be found in the historical records to support either a yes or a no answer, depending upon how you see things. Brigham Young played a remarkable geo-political game. For every move he made, he had an alternate strategy to employ. While, on the one hand, he preached the prophesy of Joseph Smith, that the US Government would fail in the upcoming Battle of Armageddon, and be replaced by a new theocracy that would rule the land; he also kept a paid lobbyist in Washington trying, without success, to get Congress to admit the State of Deseret into the Union.

Brigham Young

He had little reason to take anything but a paranoid view of the army's advance. He was there, in Missouri, exactly twenty years before, when the Mormons had been ejected from the state by military force and had never been redressed by the State, nor the Federal Government for their loss of property. Brigham had great respect for the theory of the Constitution, and its so called guaranteed protections, particularly religious freedom; but he had seen it break down in actual practice. This outlook contributed, in no small part, when he assumed leadership of the church in 1844, to the decision to lead the faithful out of the United States, and the city of Nauvoo they had founded in Illinois after being driven out of Missouri. They crossed over the border and left the United States behind, to seek out the most desolate, remote place they could find, somewhere that no one else wanted, to build their utopian kingdom. They wanted the protection and benefits of the United States, but they knew those rights would be easier to secure if the Saints, as Mormons like to call themselves, constituted a political majority. They never objected to non-Mormons living among them, so long as community standards were respected. Jew and non-Jew alike were all "Gentiles" to the Mormons. They had been settled in the Salt Lake Valley for ten years, through droughts, lean harvests, locust attacks, early frosts and a host of other natural calamities; and managed to establish a self-sufficient community of twenty or thirty thousand people, depending upon who's census you believe. However many, they definitely had created something of value; and Brigham promoted the notion that the army was coming once again, to take it all away. He broke the news to the Mormon settlers in a dramatic fashion, at a ten year anniversary party on July 24, 1857. By September, the Nauvoo Legion, as the Mormon militia was known, had deployed 800 men in the mountains, and another 400 mobilized in Salt Lake City to stop the army from entering Utah.

They adopted the military strategy that the Russians had used to defeat Napoleon, by retreating and burning the land in front of the advancing troops. The Mormons destroyed fifty-one supply wagon trains, and rustled two thirds of the military cattle, driving them to Salt Lake City; forcing the army to send contingents to New Mexico and Montana to bring back more beef for the troops. Lack of supplies was not the only factor in bringing the army to make camp at the burned-out remains of Fort Bridger, about a hundred fifty miles northeast of Salt Lake City. The road between them (now US Interstate 80) passes through Echo Canyon, a narrow defile with high cliffs on both sides. The Mormons occupied the high ground and were dug in. A few dozen men could hold off an army of thousands; and the army decided not to test that theory.

Brigham Young sent an urgent letter to the Saints in San Bernardino, advising them of the impending crisis in Utah, and encouraged them to send as many volunteers as possible to help defend Zion. It was a bring your own gun kind of affair. His supporters say he wasn't about to get driven out of Utah without a fight; but his detractors cite this as evidence that he didn't want federal troops in the territory interfering with his plans of an independent empire.

When the issue came up in San Bernardino for discussion in a general church conference as to how many

volunteers the group could afford to support for the duration of the Utah War, and who were the volunteers, the vote of the congregation was unanimous (they always are), that all the members of the congregation should volunteer to go fight. The more people, women and children, there were in Utah, the harder it would be for the military to evict them. About five hundred, half of the total membership, actually went through with it. Among that group were Fred Perris, and his two sisters, Fanny Jane, 15 and Emily 8, as well their mother, Hannah, and her husband, and new baby, Mathew Stewart Junior.

The travelling company left San Bernardino around the end of November, 1857,[24] abandoning all they couldn't carry, and hoping to get to Salt Lake City before the Battle of Armageddon broke out, or winter set in, whichever came first. They were off to fight a holy war. They had 500 revolvers.[25] The hardest part of the trip was hoisting their wagons up and over the cliff at El Cajon Pass using ropes and pulleys. Winter came early that year. They got as far as Las Vegas Springs, where they made camp until the following spring of 1858 and the mountain passes ahead of them were clear of snow.

It has been suggested that these self-appointed refugees suffered great personal and financial losses; however. Hannah Perris Stewart sold her property for $275, nearly triple what she paid for it. The value of the cabin she built on the property is unknown, nor is there any record of Fred having ever sold his lot, suggesting that it remained unimproved.

What they undertook was certainly an ordeal; but among the faithful, hardships are looked upon as a test of one's faith. Those camped out at Las Vegas that winter demonstrated that they were the true believers, ready to drop everything and answer the call of the prophet.

Well, it wasn't exactly a call, in the sense of being called to preach the word of God; but it was a demonstration of their faith. Demonstration of your faith is an important aspect of Mormonism. They had every reason to be proud of their own humility. On the other hand, about half of the Mormons in San Bernardino declined to give up their homes and move. In so doing, they proved themselves weak in the faith, and were simply excommunicated.[26]

There was a fort at Las Vegas with perhaps six permanent residents, primarily a way-station for travelers between Salt Lake and San Bernardino. It was a banner year for tourism with the 500 traveling members of the San Bernardino Ward camped out all over the meadow until Spring.

The high point of the holiday season in Las Vegas that year was December 29, when, according to LDS genealogical records, a double marriage took place.

The record says: Fred Perris married Mary Jennings on that day, while Mansfield Jennings, Mary's brother, married Fanny Jane Perris, Fred's 15 year old sister. Mansfield was 21.

Hmmm! There is a salacious story here somewhere. There always is with impromptu weddings. Double that and

you quadruple the possible directions that fictionalized story might take.

The problem with this curious historical factoid is, however, that it is only half true—or half false, depending upon how you look at it. Fanny Jane did, in fact, marry Mansfield, and bore his children.

There was no issue nor other evidence that Fred married Mary Jennings. A year and a half later, he married Mary Edwards of Cheltenham, England.[26]

Mansfield and Mary Jennings had impeccable Mormon credentials, so to speak. They were born in luxury in Memphis, Tennessee, children of a wealthy slave trader, Schuyler Jennings.[27] When he converted to Mormonism in 1848, he manumitted his slaves, and emigrated to Utah by ox cart when Mansfield was 13. Three years later they moved on to San Bernardino, and now they were returning to help establish Zion.

While Mormons incurred much wrath for their early practice of polygamy, there is no evidence that Fred ever cohabitated with more than one wife.

When the San Bernardino Ward finally broke camp in the Spring of 1858, and crossed into the Utah Territory, they were advised not to approach any closer than Springville, about 55 miles south of Salt Lake City, which was being evacuated as the advancing US Army approached from the north.

Every building in the young city was stuffed with straw and tinder; the plan being to burn the entire city to the ground, rather than leave anything for the army or the camp followers to loot. Give them barren earth, exactly as the Mormons had found it when they arrived eleven years earlier. It was the tactic the Russians had used to defeat Napoleon.

But cooler heads prevailed in this conflict. Colonel Thomas L. Kane, who recruited the Mormon Batallion, that had helped Brigham Young finance the Mormon exodus, got word of the expedition, and traveled incognito from Washington across Panama to southern California and on to Salt Lake City. He was an officer that Brigham Young trusted; and agreed to let the troops pass through the city on his promise that there would be no looting. Nonetheless the city was vacated and ready to be incinerated should any soldier break ranks. They set up camp twenty-five miles away, at Camp Floyd. The new governor, appointed by the president, to replace Brigham Young, accompanied the troops. There was no war.

By August the 30,000 residents of Salt Lake City had returned home, and picked up their lives where they had left off. The Battle of Armageddon was postponed. No refunds were given

Life returned to normal, except for the good folks from San Bernardino, who more or less got lost in the shuffle. They

needed to get crops in the ground, and not rely on the kindness of strangers, i.e. the locals, who weren't very enthusiastic about sharing their meager food supply with this many people all at once. Nor did the San Bernardino Saints like the idea of splitting up after all they had been through together; but in the end, that is what they had to do. Some settled in Springville. Fully half of them left Utah the following year, and returned to San Bernardino.[27] Of the others who stayed, some went to Chicken Creek, which was soon renamed Levan. That included the Jennings Family with Fred's sister Fanny Jane and her children. Fred went with his mother and her new Stewart Family to settle in Beaver, and pursue life as a farmer, but not for very long.

Mansfield C. Jennings 1836 - 1919

One day Mansfield Jennings, who married Fred's sister Fanny Jane, got a letter from a relative in Butte, Montana. In the letter was a want—ad, clipped from an English newspaper, placed there by the Chancery Court in Gloucester, England, seeking the heirs of Thomas Perris. Things changed for Fred. He and his sisters had inherited a fortune; but they had to go back to England to claim it.

It seems that when Hannah left Tom in Melbourne, and sailed off with the kids, he was crestfallen. Here he had conquered the world and lost all that had any meaning to him. He sold his store and all his holdings, boarded a ship, and went back home to Gloucester. Within six months he was dead.

On August 19, 1858, Fred left Beaver and traveled north to Salt Lake City, where he obtained his citizenship and a US passport. He then traveled east, keeping a daily record of his trip. He completed some kind of real estate transaction with a relative of his step-father, Mathew Stewart, in Wisconsin. He visited more Stewart relatives in Ohio; and then proceeded on to New York, boarding the steamship Thornton bound for England on the 29th of November.[28]

Mansfield Jennings found work as a teamster with a wagon company taking disillusioned Mormons back down the trail to San Bernardino. On his next trip he took along Fanny Jane, who was pregnant at the time. She gave birth to their first child in San Bernardino.

When they were able to travel, they boarded a ship to Panama, crossed over to the Atlantic side on the newly completed railroad, and proceeded on to Gloucester. All of the ocean-going vessels by this time were steam driven.

Hannah and Mathew Stewart traveled with their children, Emily and Matthew, from Beaver to Salt Lake, and then on to Ohio where she reconnected with her long, lost sister Rachel, who had fled her own wedding twenty odd years ago, leaving Hannah to marry Tom, by selling herself into bondage for seven years, to pay her passage to the New World. Working off that debt, she went on to marry a man who served a term as governor of Ohio.[29]

Hannah and Mathew left their children either with Rachel or Mathew's relatives, and proceeded on to New York and England.

Fred married his childhood sweetheart, Mary Edwards of Cheltenham (May 5, 1859).[30] The family was reunited. They retained a lawyer and presented their case to the chancery court, with Hannah speaking for her minor child, Emily who had remained in Ohio. It took more than two years to meet all the stipulations of the court and get the issue settled. For one thing, Fanny Jane was pregnant again, with a baby in her arms, and her Las Vegas marriage license wasn't considered valid. She and Mansfield were required to go through a proper English ceremony. During the long period it took for the legal machinery to grind to a court decision, Fred found work with an interesting fellow who used a complex chemical process with silver iodide and collodion to make images on a glass plate. They called it photography; and it seemed to promise some new and very enchanting possibilities.[32]

In due course the court awarded the assets of the Thomas Perris Estate, amounting to £4,000,31 to be divided among the three children, but with different payout provisions. For example, Emily could only collect her share after her 21st birthday. Apparently this was a considerable sum, even divided three ways, because the family could then go on a shopping spree on the Continent, probably Paris, where they bought furniture and clothing, as well as surveying and drafting equipment.

In the spring of 1861 they all returned to New York. By now Fanny Jane had two children. They all went at once to Ohio where they reunited with the children they hadn't seen in two years.[33]

Once again, an event far away, but not so far this time, pulled them apart. There was some kind of ruckus at a place called Fort Sumpter in South Carolina. A rebel militia had fired cannon shots at a US military base. Several states had announced they had seceeded from the Union. Newly elected President Lincoln, thinking to send federal troops to put down what proved to be an extremely well organized insurrection, found that nearly half his army was a thousand miles from the nearest railhead; and the other half had insufficient equipment and materiel with which to even fight a war. He issued a nationwide call for seventy-five thousand volunteers to "preserve the Union."

Whenever a war breaks out, first they come asking for volunteers. Then they come around looking for conscripts. Fred and brother-in-law Mansfield Jennings did not wait around to see that drama play out. They headed west with their families, arriving in Salt Lake City about the middle of August. The war was now far away. The soldiers at Camp Floyd were preparing to leave to go take part in the dreadful war between the States.

Fanny Jane and Mansfield moved first to Springville, and then on to Levan to be with the rest of the Jennings clan. They had two more children; and, after twelve years of marriage, they divorced. Fanny Jane remarried and spent the rest of her life in the largest house in town.

Fred and Mary settled in Salt Lake City, in the Seventh Ward. Their experience with urban life was considerably different from that in Levan. Nevertheless, they had a baby, and then kept having more. Over time they had six children.

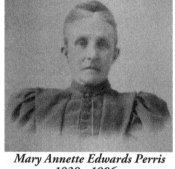

Mary Annette Edwards Perris
1839 - 1906

Fred's mother, Hannah stayed in Ohio with her husband, and new family. The war was much closer there; and when the rebel army began making rapid advances across Kentucky inflicting heavy losses on the Union soldiers, it appeared they were heading straight for Cincinnati.

A shockwave of fear swept across Ohio. Mathew Stewart joined the Ohio Volunteer Cavalry in 1862.[34] His unit crossed over into Kentucky to meet the Rebel Army. He was captured in the first battle, and sent off to the prison camp in Andersonville, South Carolina, where he died (November 1864), as did nearly all of the prisoners, of starvation and/or cholera.

When the war was over, Hannah got the news of her husband's gruesome death, and a meager government pension for his sacrifice. She moved first to Iowa, where Stewart relatives lived; and then the next season moved on to Utah. Along the way her youngest child, Herbert Stewart, died, and was buried on the plains.[35] She arrived in Salt Lake City, and lived there briefly with Fred and Mary, then moved to Levan, where Fanny Jane had finally settled.

It was a time of rapid growth and change in Salt Lake City. Every week or so, throughout the summer, a returning missionary from somewhere would arrive bringing a company of two or three hundred converts: trades-people, millwrights, carpenters and other skills, flocking in mainly from northern Europe and the Scandinavian countries particularly.

Fred's drafting and surveying skills were certainly in demand at this time; but there is no known record of exactly how he made a living. He had a camera which he presumably brought from Europe, with all the chemicals and accessories needed to make photographs, and project them with a magic lantern onto a wall. He used the process known as "Ambrotype," and showed off his works at the county fair in the summer of 1862.[36] And again, the folks in Santaquin were amused by his presentation; but apparently photography as a business enterprise wasn't too successful. Perhaps photography was just too frivolous for this strictly utilitarian society.

A telegraph line was completed to Salt Lake City. They now started getting daily news bulletins that kept the citizenry apprised of the progress of the war between the States. Johnston's Army, that had pressed its way into Utah in 1858, pulled out, but was replaced by 700 volunteers from California, under Colonel Patrick Connor. They

Main Street, Salt Lake City, 1862
Water flows in irrigation ditches on both sides of the street.

17

established Camp Douglas, (later named Fort Douglas) in the foothills overlooking the Salt Lake Valley, not only to "keep an eye on the Mormons;" but also, to keep a sharp eye out for gold or silver or any other precious minerals in the Utah mountains. They were veterans of the gold country in California; more interested in prospecting than watching over the law-abiding Mormons, who really weren't that interesting to watch anyway.

Fred was a private in the Nauvoo Legion, which was something on the order of a church-sponsored national guard. It got started originally when Joseph Smith was mayor of Nauvoo, Illinois, as an army of 5,000 soldiers to protect the city and the Saints from a repeat of the Missouri experience. Brigham Young reactivated this unit in the Salt Lake Valley, at first as a way to deal with unruly bands of native Paiutes. When Johnston's army approached Utah in 1857, this was the militia that harassed them and slowed their advance. Five years later, when Fred was enlisted, the entire command was transferred away from Brigham Young's control, to the Territorial Government. The reason for the change was because the territorial governor needed a militia to help the sheriff of Weber County enforce a court order in an astonishing incident known as the Morrisite War.[37]

Joseph Morris converted to Mormonism and emigrated to Utah in 1856. By 1862 he had been excommunicated for his proclamation that Brigham Young was a fraud, and that he, Joseph Morris, was the true prophet. He attracted a few followers, but ran into difficulties when members of his commune wanted to leave, and were being held against their will. Morris and his group had taken refuge in an abandoned fort on the Weber (WEE-bur) River, not far from Ogden. Fred was one of the two hundred fifty or so militiamen called out to help the sheriff secure the release of the prisoners. The Morrisites were prepared for a siege.

After three days of pitched battle, they raised a white flag over the compound. The sheriff and his escort were allowed to enter. In the ensuing scuffle, four people were shot dead: They were Joseph Morris and his wife, as well as John Banks, the second in command, and his wife.

The official report said the deceased were "resisting arrest;" but there were enough irregularities that the perpetrators were eventually tried in court on a charge of murder. Fred was doing guard duty a half mile away from the center of action; but he was close enough to see how excessive military force was the tool of choice to suppress any dissent in this flawed religious utopia.

Brigham Young has often been accused of combining church and state. He was, after all, both president of the church and governor of the Utah Territory at the same time; but his actions were consistent with promoting the separation of the two. Mormons give lip service to the Jeffersonian notion of a democratic republic; but the prophesies they hold sacred clearly say that all governments will fail on that "great and dreadful day." Thus, the Mormons have this continuing argument among themselves trying to define exactly where that line is, separating church and state. In their other mind they know they are both

18

ultimately the same thing. The scriptures say that governments thrive or fail, based upon God's divine purpose.

Although the people of the Territory had no vote on who would be their governor, the job was limited by how much money the Territorial Legislature gave him to spend, which wasn't much. The members of that body were elected at the ballot box from the slate of candidates selected by the School of the Prophets. More on that later.

Charles C. Rich, one of the founders of the ill-fated San Bernardino colony, was at it again, this time founding the community of Franklin on the northern border of the Utah Territory. Unfortunately, the surveyor made a little error, and the place wound up one mile north of the border in what came to be the State of Idaho.

The native Shoshones who had lived in that area for generations knew where their territory left off, and which valleys the Blackfeet occupied, as well as the Utes and the Paiutes; but they were unaware that a few lines drawn on a map somewhere far away gave Charles Rich the right to sell or give away parcels of land and erect fences around it to keep people out. Native peoples had trouble understanding the European concept of land ownership. The reports have it that the native people were friendly people — at first.

The Mormons called them their Lamanite (LAY-mun-ite) Brothers;[38] but the feelings of brotherhood soon turned sour; quite probably because the Shoshones had trouble telling the difference between wild game, which

seemed to be diminishing, and domestic livestock, which was increasing. At some point relations soured. It had to happen.

The details of what provoked the massacre are beyond the scope of this narrative; but on January 29, 1863, in subzero weather, Colonel Connor and his California Volunteers stationed in Salt Lake City, attacked a Shoshone camp on the shore of Bear Lake at dawn.

When it was all over there were 22 California Volunteers dead, 49 wounded; and 79 cases of frostbite. On the other side, there were about 225 Shoshone killed, which included 90 women and children. They called it a battle, the Battle of Bear Lake Valley.[39] It may have been the largest Indian massacre of the 19th Century, century, certainly larger than the 130 Cheyenne killed at Sand Creek the very next year, or the 146 Oglala Sioux taken out at Wounded Knee in 1890.[40] No one dared to use the word genocide.

The Mormons, of course, were not involved in the Bear Lake carnage; but once it had happened, they were quick to capitalize upon it. Three weeks after peace treaties were signed with the native tribes (July 1863), Brigham Young called Charles C. Rich on a mission to go establish a new colony in Bear Lake Valley, 46 miles over the mountain from Franklin. When asked if he knew that that area was not within the Utah Territory, Brigham replied:

"I do not know, neither do I care. We calculate to be kings of these mountains. Now let us go ahead and occupy them."[41]

19

He advised Rich that the settlers should "Lay low, and watch out for black ducks," presumably meaning federal military personnel; fearing, perhaps, that should the news of a settlement in Bear Lake Valley be telegraphed to Washington, President Lincoln might declare the land an Indian reservation, and order the military to prevent anyone else from occupying it.

For his next project, Charles C. Rich wanted a better surveyor, and called upon his old friend Fred Perris. On October 12, 1863, Fred received an appointment as Territorial Surveyor and took a crew to Bear Lake Valley, presumably doing the field work before winter set in. Somewhere between twenty and thirty families built twenty cabins with dirt floors and roofs, and spent the winter there. The following spring, 1864, Brigham Young visited the colony and liked what he saw, so much so, that he named the community for the surveyor, Fred Peris. (sic)[42]

Peris? Paris? Or is it Perris? Brigham Young was never known for his spelling. Neither was the Postal Service in Washington, D. C. for that matter. When the new community applied for a post office in Perris, Idaho, the application was issued to Paris, Idaho. The town council decided it was easier for them to amend the spelling of their town, than to change the distant bureaucracy.

Fred was now in the church leader's consciousness; and by summer he had a job working with a survey crew in Echo Canyon, the single narrow corridor through the mountains heading northeast out of Utah. The purpose of this survey was a feasibility study

to determine if, and how, a railroad track could be laid through the canyon. Five years later the Union Pacific Railroad Company did just that; but it was Brigham Young who paid for the original survey. His oldest son, Joseph, was the foreman of the crew. It was the perfect formula for disaster on the job. Fred had his own crew when he surveyed Bear Lake Valley with efficiency and accuracy. Now he had the rich owner's son giving the orders on his first job. There are any number of sub-texts that could apply to this delicate drama at the workplace. The historical fact is, Fred and the crew walked off the job in a strike. How unthinkable! How could anyone go on strike against the living Prophet of God? Well, they did, so it must have been a serious issue to them. Fred was the spokesman for the group. Possibly he was the only one who knew how to write a letter. The upshot was over payment for wages. Would they be paid in greenbacks or gold? That was the main subject of the correspondence between Fred and Brigham Young; but the back-story had to do with the conflict between on-the-job trained Fred and book-smarts Joseph who's father was the living prophet.

The Civil War dragged on. Congress in Washington ran out of money to finance the war so they started printing money on paper, which some people didn't think was worth as much as real gold. At one point the exchange rate dipped to one greenback dollar being worth only thirty nine cents in gold.[43] This caused a lot of agony in personal transactions everywhere. Brigham offered to pay his employees in greenbacks. Fred and his crew thought they had agreed on wages in gold.

In negotiations to settle the strike, Brigham's final offer was the old carrot-and-stick approach. On the one hand, he urged them to put perceived injustices aside, complete their work, and all would be well in the world. On the other hand, he considered their action "the heighth (sic) of ingratitude." After all, he went on, he had been supplying flour to their families for only 6 dollars per hundred-weight, when he could have gotten ten or twelve dollars. He closed his letter with an ominous threat that he hoped their rash actions would not "debar" them from ever finding gainful employment again.[44] Fred was a family man, with obligations. This was a difficult decision; but he stood in solidarity with his crew, refusing to go back to work until they were paid as promised. Brigham hired another survey crew, and that was the end of the strike; and the end of Fred's career. The railroad was laid down the canyon and across the territory a few years later, with lots and lots of work for civil engineers; but

there is no evidence that Fred ever participated in any way. Brigham Young held the exclusive contract to provide labor for the project. He came to own a considerable bloc of Union Pacific Railroad stock.

Fred was unemployed—but not for long. There is never an idle hand in a Mormon community. Some jobs don't pay as well as others, but there's always work. In 1865 he was a police clerk. He got on well with the Chief of Police, and was appointed Captain of the 7th Ward in a special police unit that was attempting to build a network of operatives throughout the city. He became secretary of the group, and watched with dismay as it took on an increasingly secret and conspiratorial nature.

Random assassinations began to occur. He had reason to suspect members of the organization, and wrote how he gradually pulled away from it. Years later, wishing to forget the whole shady

Fred T. Perris, a commission buyer for George Cronyn, 1866

episode, he became greatly agitated when members of the ring were being prosecuted, for fear he too would be dragged into court and compelled to testify about the whole unsavory episode.[45]

The following year, 1866, Fred was working for George Cronyn a merchant on West Temple Street, dealing in "dry-goods and groceries."[46] Fred's job was to make trips east as a commission buyer. He earned praise for his honesty and integrity in his dealings.[47] In New York he made the acquaintance of another buyer from Salt Lake City, William S. Godbe, a merchant with a line of credit up to a quarter of a million dollars. His friendship with Godbe played a significant role in the political history of Utah.

Fred prospered in his job with George Cronyn, expanding the company in new directions. For example, Fred purchased the parts, and apparently assembled the first steam-driven, fine lumber mill in the Salt Lake Valley, so that doors, cabinets, and furniture could be made locally.[48] It was good times with an expanding economy. By 1868 the Salt Lake Register listed Fred T. Perris as employed by Cronyn & Perris, on West Temple Street. He had bought into the company, and found a new career.

By outward appearance the Mormon Zion of Salt Lake City was a success. It survived and it grew; but inwardly it didn't turn out to be the utopian society its founding pioneers had set out to create. Nothing ever succeeds as planned, of course;[49] but it didn't even come close. The Mormon ideal

of small, self sufficient communities, living close to the land, with little or no need for outside products or influence has proven to work better among the Amish of Pennsylvania than among the Mormons of Utah. From the very beginning, Salt Lake City was a commercial hub. Money was always the medium of exchange. Times were good when there was plenty of it around. Times were tough when there wasn't; and the first to be blamed were the greedy Gentile merchants.

Brigham Young had little use for retail stores. They produced nothing. He allowed them because he couldn't really stop them. He viewed them as economic siphons, sucking away what little hard currency there was in the Territory, and sending it back east, in exchange for such useless products as tobacco, liquor, coffee, tea, and "fashionable clothing."

At least George Cronyn and Fred Auerbach had their shops over on the side street, where the better people seldom went; so they weren't quite as offensive to Brigham Young as the brash and audacious eyesore on Main Street called Walker Bros. General Store. There wasn't a preacher in the valley worth his Sunday sermons, who couldn't relate every problem in the Territory to those apostate merchants, Joseph, Samuel, David, and Matthew Walker, sons of an English squire said to have been of "considerable landed estate."

The Walker Brothers converted to Mormonism and emigrated to Salt Lake in about 1852. They were faithful to the Church, and moderately successful businessmen, until they incurred Brigham's wrath in 1858, by defying his ban on selling supplies to the US Army. It was a Church edict only, not the government, since Brigham was no longer the territorial governor. The Walker Brothers took it as a market opportunity. They made money because there were no other vendors supplying food to the quartermaster. Brigham Young threatened to excommunicate them, and then carried through with it; but it didn't affect their government contract at all. Eventually the church leader realized how his own edict had created the monopoly, and rescinded the ban; but by then it was too late. The Walkers had made their fortune; and were forevermore a political and social thorn in Brigham's side. They were living proof that a man could prosper in Utah, even receive a generous share of the "material blessings of heaven," without the sanction of the Church.[50]

The Saints were admonished to avoid the Walker Brothers; but their store prospered in spite of Brigham Young.

All he really achieved with his numerous sermons against them was free advertising from the pulpit

The problem of what to do about the Walker Bros', and the other Gentile stores, was discussed at great length by the School of the Prophets. This was not a school, as such, but more of a town hall meeting, or public forum, that met every Saturday afternoon in the Tabernacle, conducted by Brigham Young. It wasn't fully public. Attendance was restricted to brethren who were "in good standing" with the Church, meaning those who sustained Brigham Young as a living prophet of God. Women, of course, were never in attendance, so it was something less than a democratic institution; but it was a meeting of the village elders, about a thousand men, and they acted upon a variety of issues, economic and political. They selected the list of candidates to be placed on the ballot and voted upon for all public offices, from city commissioners to territorial legislators. One solution they came

The Mormon Tabernacle 1868

23

up with for the problem of too much currency flowing out of the Territory was to persuade everyone to take a wage cut, which would thus make the cost of imported goods coming from back east, relatively more expensive.[51] It was the old balance-of-trade problem. They selected members of their group, representatives of each of the trades, to call meetings, and address their fellow trades-people, and convince them to support this idea for the overall betterment of society. For some reason the program was never successfully implemented. But they gave it a try.

Another brilliant proposal was to boycott all the Gentile stores. That was easier said than done. Finally the School of the Prophets hit upon the scheme of establishing a competitive store, a Mormon co-op, that would supply everything that Walker Bros' had, but manufactured locally by Mormon hands. They named their venture Zion's Cooperative Mercantile Institute, capitalized at $1,000,000. It opened its doors on March 1, 1869, for the sole purpose of driving the Walkers Brothers into bankruptcy.

ZCMI was an instant success; and continued for a hundred years as a publicly traded corporation. Sales at the Walker Store dropped from $60,000 per month to $5,000;[52] but not all of that drop could be attributed to the success of the Mormon retail venture. An economic panic swept across the Utah Territory in 1869, not because of retailing, but due to railroad shenanigins.

The Union Pacific Railroad had contracted with Brigham Young to supply all the labor needed to lay track across the territory. He could extract that kind of a contract from the railroad company, because his position as religious leader gave him a kind of union boss power to control the labor supply. Was the contract with Brigham Young, or the Church? It was hard to tell the difference. The transcontinental railroad was completed. Then the railroad company defaulted on its contract to pay one million dollars in back wages. Workers went unpaid. Brigham Young got blamed. Merchants who had extended credit were forced into bankruptcy Although sales at Walker Bros' dropped precipitously, they survived the panic by moving into the banking business. They continued to thrive as a business entity for another century as Walker Bank and Trust, until merging with First Interstate Bank in the 1970's.

Cronyn and Perris on West Temple Street was not as fortunate as the Walker Brothers. They were forced to close their doors in bankruptcy. Fred was unemployed again.

Brigham Young was financially involved in a majority of the business ventures in the Territory. Whichever way the economy turned, he continued to amass wealth. He built a stately home for his several dozen wives and 50 or so children. Others lived in abject poverty. Some people said an economic system that enhances one man at the expense of others was not what the founder of Mormonism had intended. Opposition to Brigham's autocracy began to mount. There was a good deal of lawlessness at the time. This was the gun-toting period of the Old

West, when there were a lot of Civil War veterans roaming around who had run out of war, but were still itching for a fight. A genre of Hollywood films is based upon this moment in history

In October 1869, Fred landed a job - a real, civil engineering job. It wasn't a big one: only five miles of narrow-gauge track to run from Coalville to the mouth of Echo Canyon.[53]

Coalville is about 35 miles east of Salt Lake City over a high mountain pass. The project was to ship coal north to the transcontinental railroad, and from there to Ogden, and on to Salt Lake City along the Utah Central Railroad, which track had been laid earlier in the summer using all volunteer labor. W. W. Cluff, the bishop in Coalville, hoped to do the same thing with the Coalville and Echo Canyon Railroad Co, offering company stock in exchange for labor. There was money to be made shipping coal to Salt Lake City.

William S. Godbe

The rail and the other materials were to come from the surplus left over after the completion of the transcontinental railroad. The Union Pacific, in its race to build the line, intentionally shipped an excess of materials, which was cheaper than to run the risk of construction being slowed down for lack of rail or ties. The Church acquired possession of these surplus items in its million-dollar lawsuit against Union Pacific for failure to pay back wages

In the first of week of October Bishop Cluff threw an elaborate ground-breaking ceremony with a brass band, signing up stockholder/laborers. Bringing a railroad to town was a big deal. Fred was there. He and Fewson Smith were essentially the management team for this enterprise; so there was probably some salary promised, plus stock, of course. Bishop Cluff passed around lots of that to get things going.

Despite his job out of town, however, Fred was back home in Salt Lake City on Saturday, October 23, 1869, the date of an important turning point in his life. This was the eruption of a conflict known as the Godbe Heresy, named for his friend, William S Godbe, the merchant.

In contrast to the Morrisite affair when he was on the outskirts of the action, this time Fred was in the very thick of it, even, for a period, the leading spokesman of the movement that grew out of this incident.

Godbe had been a bishop. The office of bishop, as the head of a ward, in the Mormon structure, is a lay position, but it entails far more than simply an ecclesiastical office. The job is very nearly a full time occupation, oftentimes taking more of a man's time than his regular job, which he must maintain, of course, because the office of bishop doesn't pay. A bishop can get reimbursed for expenses; but it is volunteer service.

25

Bishop Godbe was also a deeply spiritual man; that is to say: he was deeply into spiritualism. He and a traveling companion, Elias L. T. Harrison, attended a number of séances in New York City, and communicated with the departed spirits of Mormon leaders, including Heber C. Kimball, the recently deceased First Counselor to Brigham Young.[54] They presented a list of questions to the spirit, to test its authenticity, and wrote down the answers they received. They returned to Salt Lake City firm in the knowledge of what they must do to reform the Church.

With Harrison as editor, and Godbe as publisher, they began publishing The Utah Magazine, a monthly periodical with a liberal slant, by writers named Tullidge, Stenhouse, Kelsey, and Shearman to mention a few. A coterie of intellectuals soon began to collect around Bishop Godbe. They called themselves "The New Movement," and hung out around the university up on the east bench with the intellectuals and free-thinkers, a dangerous practice to be sure. A lot of stalwart Mormons said it was just the same old movement they had seen before, the first step to apostasy, when someone starts to "criticize the Prophet" or the Church.

Speaking of apostasy however, two brothers, Alexander and David Smith, sons of the Mormon founder, Joseph

E. L. T. Harrison

Smith Jr. (1805-44), came to town one day as missionaries, proclaiming that the true Church of Jesus Christ of Latter Day Saints, the one that their father, the Prophet Joseph had restored to the Earth, had been reorganized, and was now under the leadership of Joseph Smith III, eldest son of the Prophet, who had been ordained by his father to be his true successor.

Unfortunately the father died of gunshot wounds at a protest rally while the ordained successor was still a boy. Had it not been for Brigham Young at that crucial moment, as the ranking member of the Quorum of Twelve Apostles, stepping forward with his genius ability at organizing, and moving the faithful to a safer place, there would be no Church at all. It would have been dispersed. Now that that boy had grown to maturity and gained some experience in the world, he was ready to assume his calling as the true leader of the Church. Brigham had done many wonderful things, the Smith Brothers conceded; but if he now refused to step aside for the true successor, that was evidence in itself that power had corrupted him, so that now he was leading the Church astray. It was Brigham, they said, who started the vile practice of polygamy, not Joseph Smith. Furthermore, the Prophet Joseph had said the gathering place for the Saints in these the last days, was Jackson County, Missouri, not Utah.

Those things may seem trivial in retrospect; but the issue, who is the true president, reverberated across the Territory for months, coming close to violence on a number of occasions. There were the Josephites and the Brighamites, both just looking for a good excuse. to pummel the opposition. Finally the tension was resolved when a company of several hundred persons packed up, and with Colonel Connor's military escort, to assure them a safe exit, left Utah and emigrated to Missouri.

The Utah Magazine thrived by taking a neutral editorial position, trying to act as the impartial umpire in this debate, giving equal emphasis to both sides. So long as they limited themselves to issues no more controversial than that, Brigham Young gave his tacit approval to the publication. The first time the magazine took an editorial stand against any Church action was when the School of the Prophets tried to talk down wages in the Territory as a way to improve the trade balance. Harrison, the editor, predicted it would not work; and of course, it didn't.

Devout Mormons took note of this accelerating pace of apostasy. Next, the magazine took a position in favor of developing the mining industry in the Territory as a way to infuse cash into the perennially depressed economy.

Joseph Smith Jr.
Founder of the LDS movement

Brigham Young's response was, that while he couldn't forbid anyone from digging for "precious metals", the Saints hadn't needed them in the early days, and they didn't need them now; and besides, he argued, most of the mining claims were held by Gentiles, which would never do the Saints any good anyway. The real issue, critics said, was the increased frequency with which the magazine leveled criticisms at the Prophet. Throughout all of this intellectual ferment, Fred Perris maintained a close friendship with William Godbe. His thinking must have paralleled many of the issues raised by the Utah Magazine.

The publication finally found the limit of Brigham's patience when it challenged the basic assumption of Mormon theology by printing:

There is one fatal error, which possesses the minds of some, it is this: that God Almighty intended the priesthood to do our thinking. Our own opinion is that, when we invite men to use free speech and free thought to get into the Church, we should not call upon them, or ourselves, to kick down the ladder by which they and we ascended to Mormonism. They should be called upon to think on as before, no matter who has or has not thought in the same direction. Think freely, and think forever. [55]

That did it. Brigham promptly called Harrison, the editor of the magazine, on a mission; and he probably called Bishop Godbe on the carpet. He also called other members of the editorial staff on missions, as a way to disperse the group. They each refused the calls, of course, thus revealing the full scope of their dwindling faith. Their unwillingness to live the principle of obedience; in open defiance of the sacred vows they had each taken, demonstrated that there was some serious repentance that needed to be done. Brigham chose the weekly Saturday afternoon meeting of the School of the Prophets to give these brethren the opportunity to do just that. He called upon Bishop Godbe first, and then on Harrison to stand before the assemblage and explain themselves before the Elders of Zion, one thousand strong in the Tabernacle. Neither of them were in attendance. This agitated the group, and Brigham proceeded to ask them if there were any reason why these two brethren, who's civic duty it was to be here in attendance, should not, here and now, be disfellowshipped. Unlike Roberts Rules of Order, motions from the chair are quite permissible in Mormon parliamentary procedure. In an effort to show his benevolent side, Brigham agreed to postpone the vote to the next meeting, a week later.

There is a difference between disfellowshipped and excommunication. In the first case the dissident is still allowed to pay his or her tithing, and thus continue receiving the "blessings of heaven" as promised by the Prophet Malachi. In the latter case his or her name is removed from the Church records and that eternal soul is turned over to "the buffetings of Satan."[56]

Godbe and Harrison were present at the next meeting, as were all of their friends and supporters, including Fred Perris, who made the trip back from Coalville for this momentous occasion when Bishop Godbe got the opportunity to present his case for the "new movement."

After Godbe finished speaking, Brigham rebutted with "aggravating mimicry, turning everything into ridicule."[57] Harrison spoke next. Throwing all caution to the wind, he answered Brigham's crudeness with defiance. When he finished, Brigham arose, not to put the question to the assembly, but rather to announce that these brethren had not shown the proper spirit of repentance, and thus the motion was changed. It would be not whether they should or should not be disfellowshipped. Rather, the motion was to turn them over to an excommunication court to be convened on the following Monday.

In Mormon parliamentary procedure, a motion begins: "It is proposed that . . ." followed by whatever the issue might be, concluding with: "All in favor may signify by the raising of the right hand."

In every Mormon election, and they occur several times a year, this vote is always unanimous, with every right hand in the congregation raised in perfect, silent unison.

The speaker continues. "All opposed may signify by the same sign." After a moment's pause he will report: "The voting has been unanimous."

It always is. There have been few instances since the founding of the Church in 1830, when there has ever been a single dissenting vote. This Saturday afternoon was one of those rare occasions.

Brigham asked the question. "All in favor may signify by the raising of the right hand." A thousand right hands went up.

"All opposed?"

It was the moment of truth for the "new movement." They stepped forth to test the greatest right guaranteed by the U.S. Constitution, the right to dissent. They raised their hands in silent opposition. How many were involved? That is hard to estimate. Perhaps a dozen. It seems unlikely there were more. All those present, after all, had tickets to get in; and you couldn't get a ticket if you were any kind of a trouble maker.

Brigham Young paused long enough to let everyone see who the dissenters were, and undoubtedly to let someone make a note of their names. Mormons record an amazing amount of information. On Monday, as promised, the High Council convened. Godbe and Harrison were duly excommunicated. Harrison delivered an impassioned defense at his trial; but nobody listened. He published his statement in The Utah Magazine; but by then the magazine had already received it's death blow.

The next issue of the Deseret Evening News printed a letter from Brigham Young to all the Saints:

Our attention has been called of late to several articles which have appeared in The Utah Magazine . . . An examination of them has convinced us that they are erroneous, opposed to the spirit of the Gospel, and calculated to do injury. According to the practice of the Church, teachers were sent to labor with the editor and publishers, to point out to them the evil results which would follow a persistence in the course they are pursuing. This did not have the desired effect, and they have since been tried before the High Council, and after a thorough and patient investigation of the case, it was found they had imbibed the spirit of apostasy to a degree that they could not any longer be fellowshiped (sic) and they were cut off from the Church. The Utah Magazine is a periodical that in its spirit and teachings is directly opposed to the work of God. Instead of building up Zion and uniting the people, its teachings, if carried out, would destroy Zion, divide the people asunder, and drive the Holy Priesthood from the earth.

Therefore, we say to our Brethren and Sisters in every place, The Utah Magazine is not a periodical suitable for circulation among, or perusal by them, and should not be sustained by Latter day Saints. We hope this will be sufficient, without ever having to refer to it again. [58]

It had been a tumultuous weekend for Fred, witnessing a momentous defeat for "the new movement." He went back to his job in Coalville with a better understanding of why there is seldom a dissenting vote in a Mormon election. The subject of whether Fred should come before a church court for his rash action in supporting Godbe came up for discussion between the bishop of the 7th Ward and his counselors. So long as he was working out of town, there wasn't much they could do.

Within a matter of days after Fred got back to work, W. W. Cluff, as president of the Coalville and Echo Canyon Railroad, stopped all construction abruptly, locked the office door, and left town, having been called on a mission. It is unclear whether Fred was ever paid for his work or not.

And he was out of work again. It is hard to imagine that he didn't feel some sense of persecution. If he weren't closely associated with the "new movement" before, he certainly was by now. As autocrats always do, he reasoned, Brigham Young had created his own opposition in the cavalier manner by which he had approached his dissenters. Neither Godbe nor Harrison wanted to leave the Church. They sought to improve it. In the long run, they did exactly that, demonstrating once again that the LDS Church is more malleable to change from outside pressure than from within.[59] Where there is no dissent, there can be no change.

It turned out that Fred was wrong in his assumption that the railroad project had been terminated because of his dissenting vote. Brigham was not acting vindictively. It was undoubtedly a cold business decision that Cluff made when he learned (maybe from

insider information that he got from stockholder Brigham Young) that the Union Pacific Railroad, which owned land for ten miles on both sides of the track, had discovered coal on their property near Rock Springs, Wyoming, reportedly of a better quality than Utah coal. This meant that the railroad company with a monopoly control over the track, and with no restrictions, could set the freight charge so high that Coalville coal couldn't compete with Rock Springs coal. The Coalville and Echo Canyon Railroad was doomed to failure before the track was ever laid.

It is possible that Brigham Young called Cluff on a mission to test his faithfulness after learning that Cluff had hired a troublemaker like Fred Perris; but that may be drifting into the popular trap of confusing circumstance with conspiracy. In any event, Fred's name was on a watch list. The Church archives have a private letter from one of the Apostles to Brigham Young, listing the "apostate troublemakers that should be watched."[60] Among them he named Fred T. Perris.

Fred was back in town, and looking for a job, while Bishop McLellend, bishop of the Seventh Ward was looking for a way to deal with the matter of Fred's membership in the Church. Fred was no longer able to obtain a ticket to attend the School of the Prophets meetings. The bishop sent teachers, and even went himself with his two counselors to work with Fred and Mary to help them see the error of their ways and repent.

The issue was settled at a meeting on the evening of January 21, 1870. The Church archives have a handwritten report:, the minutes of a meeting of the block teachers. When the topic of Fred T. Perris was brought up, the bishop admitted to visiting him, and finding no change, that he was still "finding fault with President Young." The bishop had no choice but to recommend excommunication for Fred and Mary. The vote to sustain that recommendation was unanimous.

The first thing William Godbe did after his excommunication was to organize The Church of Zion, and begin holding regular meetings. A great many people attended, including several of Brigham Young's wives. Their presence gave Godbe a kind of legitimacy that helped dispel threats of violence or mob action that were so prevalent at the time. In the end, religious toleration prevailed, though Godbe's church did not.

Old time apostates like Joseph R. Walker, who had thrived for years without Brigham's blessings, had little patience with Godbe and his unrelenting piety and egocentrism. What was the point, he contended, of replacing one theocracy with another?

On the other hand, Godbe had little use for Walker; who was only in it for the money. Nevertheless, it was Fred Perris who fulfilled the role of negotiator here, bringing these two men, and their supporters together, as they groped their way toward organizing an effective opposition.

Meaningful political action, they all agreed, required an organ, a publication to get the message out; but what to do, now that Brigham had essentially killed The Utah Magazine?

Simple solution. Publish The Utah Tribune. If Brigham didn't like the Magazine, he was sure to hate the Tribune. They counted on there being enough like-minded people out there to support an anti-establishment publication. While they were at it, they decided to change the format from a monthly magazine to a weekly newspaper, and take on the Church-owned *Deseret Evening News*,

The result was that on January 1, 1870 the first issue of T*he Mormon Tribune* rolled off the press. E. L. T. Harrison, was the editor. He insisted the word 'Mormon" be in the masthead as a reminder that despite all the changes in format, this was still a spiritual publication. Fred apparently worked as the accountant or at least bookkeeper for the enterprise.

By February 1870 the Godbeites and the Walkerites were firmly united; and, along with a few Irish miners and some Greek sheepherders, they held a convention in the Masonic Lodge, and organized the Liberal Party of Utah, with a party platform opposing polygamy as well as "the union of Church and State." They came out in favor of mining as an industry to promote; and affirmed their dedication to the US Constitution, as well as the laws passed by Congress. They called for "perfect freedom" in all religious matters; but went on to assert that:

The practices of the established Church of Utah . . . in its assumption of an infallible priesthood constitutes a theocracy, which, by usurping the authority to direct in temporal matters,

becomes a despotism subversive
of every right and privilege of a
free people.[61]

They also nominated a full slate of
candidates for all the offices available
in the upcoming municipal election,
including the name of Fred T.
Perris, for one of the city council seats of
Salt Lake City. Many of the Saints
were not accustomed to the presence
of a dissenting political party in their
midst, and were very upset by its
appearance. They had traveled a long
road of tears and sacrifice from Ohio to
Missouri to Illinois and finally to Utah
to build their kingdom, far away from
all political strife and contention. They
looked upon these upstart Liberals as
the worst element in town, and found
their parades and political rallies
threatening.

A number of people were certain that
military action of some sort would be
needed to keep the anticipated violence
under control. That nothing did break
out may, in some small part, have been
due to the presence of the G.L.U. The
G L U, or Gentile League of Utah,
was organized by George R. Maxwell,
who appointed himself general of
the private militia. Anyone against
Brigham Young was a friend of General
Maxwell, who took to the Liberal Party
as his own, whether they wanted him or
not. At one political rally on the street,
where Fred and his political allies were
trying to present themselves to the
public, Mormon hecklers became too
numerous for any of the speakers to go
on. General Maxwell took to the stand,
said he had had enough of this disorder,
and called for his G.L.U.'s to restore
order. At that point one hundred men

stepped out of the crowd, and formed a
semicircle behind the speaker with their
guns drawn on the audience, prepared
to shoot anyone who interrupted the
proceedings. The speaker was then
allowed to go on. This tactic may not
have garnered a lot of votes, but it did
keep the peace.

The People's Party spoke for the
Church and religious values. Their
candidates were all prominent Church
leaders, who campaigned on a theme
of preserving religious values. There
were about 20,000 votes cast on that
election day in the spring of 1870, with
1,000 going for the Liberal Party, and
the balance for the Church-sponsored
People's Party. Brigham Young
undoubtedly looked upon the vote as
a crushing defeat for the Liberals; but
Fred and the other defeated candidates
celebrated their victory in having
created a real, two party election, the
first in the territory. The next year
they nominated and campaigned for a
delegate to Congress.

One of the objections Congress had to
admitting Utah into the Union was that
it was ruled by a single party. In an effort
to overcome that objection, Brigham
Young acted in the only way he knew
how, by creating a two party system.
He decreed at a School of the Prophets
meeting that all the brethren on one side
of the congregation would henceforth be
Democrats, and all those on the other side
would become Republicans.[62] Although
many Utah families still trace their
political party allegiance back to this
incident, it was toward a more secular
basis, and the activists found themselves
torn by conflicts and squabbling.
Fred was in there, as always, looking

for the middle ground, trying find a compromise, and to hold antagonistic factions of the disintegrating "New Movement" together.

Joseph R. Walker agreed to finance the publication, if they could find a new editor, and turn it from a weekly into a daily newspaper. They hired Oscar W. Sawyer, a seasoned newspaper man from *The New York Herald*; and on April 15, 1871, the first issue of *The Salt Lake Daily Tribune and Utah Mining Gazette* came rolling off the press, with both guns drawn on Brigham Young, and his "polygamic (sic) theocracy". In the masthead were the names Godbe, Harrison, and Shearman, with Sawyer as the editor. A month later, on May 23rd, the masthead changed slightly with the addition of a fifth name: Fred T. Perris, Assistant Business Manager.[63] It was a well written newspaper, and well received in the community.

Historians attribute its survival to the simple fact that it was an unusually good newspaper in such a rough and tumble, unexpected place. It was devoted to much more than just criticism of Church leadership. It covered local events not sponsored by the Church, and news from the outlying districts, including the non-Mormon mining towns. Gentiles and Saints alike read the "Trib"; though few of the latter would ever admit it.

Yet the very success of *The Tribune* exacerbated the dissentions and conflicts among its founders. The big showdown came at a meeting of the Tribune board of directors in July 1871. The factions could no longer be reconciled. Harrison, the former editor,

denounced Oscar Sawyer, the current editor, and the direction he had taken the publication. It was never intended to be an organ of the radicals, nor of the outright enemies of the Mormon people, he said. Sawyer was wrong when he allowed a federal judge to write editorials in support of his own judicial decisions at the bench. Sawyer had to go! Sawyer went—only too glad to return to New York. Six months in Utah was enough for him. But there was no going back for *The Tribune*. It had a readership, and a reputation to uphold. Joseph R. Walker threatened to pull his advertising if Harrison took over the job as editor. Shearman disappeared, taking a trip to the States. Harrison and Godbe remained united, and when one left, the other went too, leaving no one to run the newspaper except the office staff and the Assistant Business Manager; so, beginning July 22, 1871, the single name on the masthead of the *Salt Lake Tribune* was F. T. Perris, Business Manager, published by the Tribune Publishing Company Inc., comprised of leading businessmen of this city." It was a courageous act in those turbulent times when men carried guns on their hips. There were frequent assassinations and people disappearing right off the streets.

From *The Tribune* of January 16, 1873:

A man named John Dale, resident of the 7th ward, left home last Sunday a week ago about 10 o'clock a.m., to go to a meeting, and has not been heard from since. He left a wife and six children.

Query—Has he sloped [sic], got killed, been shaded by the

'Danites, or been devoured by the G.L.U.s? Or is it not a genuine case of elopement?

The Danites were a secret band of avenging angels that lurked throughout the Mormon community for about 40 years.[64] Their actions, and indeed their very existence, was, and still is, hotly disputed. By publicizing incidents such as these, however, *The Tribune* helped provoke Federal prosecutions that finally brought these mysterious occurrences to an end. Years later, in a rare moment when Fred referred to this period in his life, he said it wasn't the death threats against him personally that bothered him, as much as it was the ones made against his wife and children.[65]

Hans Huth, a German convert who immigrated to Utah in this period, wrote:

People frequently disappear and usually the Indians are reported as their abductors or murderers, Those who disappear are usually such as are acquainted with secrets, who reveal them to the uninitiated, and who cannot keep silent. For this reason I was never ever inquisitive. I know that I cannot very well keep silent either, and I was still fond of living. I could write a great deal about these disappearances, but—(sic)—[66]

Thomas Stenhouse, writing of the period said the Parrish Family was murdered while trying to escape from Springville.[67]

He and Edward Tullidge, who also wrote an extensive history of the period, were the principal reporters for *The Tribune* under Fred's stewardship, but their names seldom appeared. They covered the notorious arrest of Brigham Young on 16 Federal counts of "lascivious cohabitation;" as well as all the devious twists and legal maneuvers the lawyers on both sides used in court, as the law of the land came face to face with the religious law of polygamy. There was never a mention of any of this famous lawsuit in the Church owned *Deseret News*. It was something of a joke that a matter so important went unreported.

When Brigham Young's fifty-first wife, Ann Eliza, filed for divorce, *The Tribune* covered every scandal-laden word of the event. At the time of the marriage she was 23. He was 67. If you had read only *The Deseret Evening News*, you would have never known it happened.

The Tribune, under Fred's stewardship waged a campaign urging the President of the United States to appoint Joseph R. Walker as Territorial Governor. That may seem a little self-serving by today's journalistic standards, to see an editorial extolling the virtues of the man who paid for the advertising in the very next column.

Walker never served as governor. Not every cause the newspaper championed was successful. But Walker continued to support Fred, and likewise, *The Tribune's* advertising probably saved his store in the face of the ZCMI competition.

In a direct challenge to the popular notion that the School of the Prophets was some kind of democratic institution, Fred, in his editorials pressed for the right of Tribune reporters to cover the Saturday afternoon meetings. Rather than allow any dissenters into his precious meeting who might challenge his authority, Brigham Young disbanded the meetings entirely. Started by Joseph Smith, and utilized by Brigham Young, this quasi-governmental body became anachronistic as Mormonism evolved from Smith's vision of a socialistic theocracy, ruled by one man, into the mainstream thinking on the unique roles of church and state in society. It wasn't that Fred's editorial urgings changed the Mormon leader's head. It gave him an opportunity to discard what wasn't working anymore in his efforts to clarify the church/state problem; and at the same time outsmart that renegade newspaper.

The Tribune opposed the admission of Utah into the Union until the political power of the Church was broken. Separation of church and state was the background music for this political theatre and. it found a receptive audience. Circulation increased. A liberal sentiment developed, particularly around the university. People talked about issues they had never dared mention before.

The last gambit to insure that LDS values remained in force throughout the Territory, as Brigham Young, step by step, removed the Church from the political process, was to persuade the LDS members of the Territorial Legislature to pass legislation granting suffrage rights to women. Fred and his newspaper opposed that as a thinly veiled attempt to keep the Mormons in

charge by increasing the voting power of families with multiple wives, three or four; or, in Brigham Young's case, twenty seven or fifty one or perhaps seventy, depending on who's version of history you want to accept.

Fred and his writers were on the wrong side of history with that one. Their campaign to repeal women's suffrage never went anywhere. Utah rightly deserves the credit for being first in the nation to extend voting rights to women. The downside to extending that right was that women didn't always vote the way men hoped they would.

The Tribune extolled the virtues of Utah, with its stability and reliable labor force, as a good place for eastern capitalists to invest. But outside capital is always slow to flow where it cannot influence the political agenda. Utah evolved into two semi-hostile political camps, where it remains pretty much unchanged to this day: roughly divided along the liberal/conservative fault line, two sides forever contentious, forever suspicious of each other's motives.

The Tribune thrived, but managing it took a heavy toll on Fred. It wasn't his passion. He had more or less fallen into this profession out of necessity. Now at age 36, and not a fighter by nature, he seems to have started looking for a way to get out. In July 1873 he sold the newspaper abruptly.

Because he gave such a favorable price, it has been assumed he and the operation were close to bankruptcy. Perhaps it was. More accurately, however, he may have given it away when he felt he had found the right team to carry on the cause: three journalists from Kansas. If anything, the editorial policy became even more strident than before Fred's departure.

On the 24th of July 1873, his final editorial appeared:

With this number terminates my connection with The Tribune as its manager. It is unnecessary to state the reasons leading to such a change, suffice it to say that the directors of the Tribune Printing & Publishing Company have been satisfied with my conduct of the paper, and that the change is necessary to me, and may not retard the welfare of the paper I have aided in establishing. To the public I would say that I have done the best I could; when all circumstances are truthfully considered. I therefore, owe it no apology, and I trust that at least the greater portion owes me no ill will. Pecuniarily (sic) I shall be benefited by the change, and the cause of religious emancipation in Utah will continue. If in the past I have contributed to this consummation my labors have not been in vain, and I can give the assurance that my future course will be in the same direction.

I cannot sever my connection without expressing publicly my appreciation of the services and kindly relations which have existed between myself and the employees of the office —"editorial staff," "typos," and "press-men" inclusive—all of whom have not only done their duty, but have even manifested

that kindly regard which will remain ineffacable (sic).

As The Tribune in the future will be conducted by strangers to the Territory and to myself, I cannot say what its course will be.

Bidding the public a journalistic good-bye,

I still respectfully remain,

Fred T. Perris

Several days later he left town, never to return, taking his wife and family, (three children), and all that he possessed with him, including the printing press used to print The Tribune. (The new publishers had their own press.) Fred and his family moved south about 120 miles to Levan, where his mother had been living, raising her younger children. She never remarried. His sister, Fanny Jane had also been living there for the past dozen years. After four children and eleven years of marriage, she divorced Mansfield, and remarried Joseph Wilson, spending the rest of her life with him.

The following Spring, of 1874, Fred and Mary set off down the Old Pioneer Trail with their children and belongings, arriving in San Bernardino by summer. His mother and her children left Levan about the same time, traveling north through Salt Lake City to the transcontinental railroad, which they took to San Francisco, and then a steamship to Southern California, where they reunited with Fred and his Family in San Bernardino.[67]

He reclaimed possession of the property he had purchased so many years before;

and within a couple of years built a spacious home which he and Mary occupied for the rest of their lives.

Shortly after his arrival, Fred set up his printing press and began printing advertising.[68] He sold his interest in that venture when he received an offer to go to work as the County Surveyor of San Bernardino County, He and his crew surveyed the entirety of this, the largest county in all of the United States, which of course includes Death Valley. He laid out proposed dam sites in the San Bernardino mountains and water distribution systems. From there he accepted work with the Atchison, Topeka, and Santa Fe Railroad, rising quickly to the position of chief engineer. In that capacity, he and 6,000 laborers completed the second transcontinental railroad, laying track from Barstow to San Bernardino through the once impossible El Cajon Pass that not so many years before could only be scaled by block and tackle. He surveyed a string of towns south of Riverside, one of which was named for him.

His sister, Emily lived with their mother until the age of 45, when she married Thomas Jefferson Evans, age 73, pioneer in the valley, father of seven children, and older than his mother-in-law, Hannah.[69] who couldn't stand him. She left San Bernardino, returning once again to Levan where she spent her last years with her other daughter, Fanny Jane. accomplishments in Southern California are outside the scope of this publication. Suffice it to say that he had a long and productive career as a surveyor and civil engineer. He is remembered there, by a number of landmarks, including the Perris Hill Municipal Park on land he donated to the City of San Bernardino, as well as the City of Perris in Riverside County.

It is unfortunate that his contributions in Utah have been largely ignored. Nevertheless, *The Salt Lake Tribune,* as well as the misspelled City of Paris, Idaho, exist as unacknowledged tributes to the talented Fred T. Perris in Deseret.
♦

Fred T. Perris and Family 1901

NOTES and REFERENCES

1) The Mormon Church or LDS Church, headquartered in Salt Lake City, has vast corporate holdings, including controlling interests in major institutions in such diverse industries as banking, airlines, manufacturing, and retailing. It is continually readjusting its investment portfolio, and is reputed to have an income in excess of one million dollars a day. Because the editorial policy of *The Salt Lake Tribune* has become so conciliatory toward the Church in recent decades, it is often suspected that the Church acquired a secret controlling interest of its erstwhile arch enemy.

2) *The Salt Lake Tribune*, July 22, 1871-July 24, 1873. The masthead lists: F. T. Perris, Business Manager, "published by the Tribune Publishing Company, incorporated, comprised of leading business men of this city." (microfilms found in the Marriott Library, University of Utah, Salt Lake City)

3) Heritage Tales, 1979, Second Annual Publication of the City of San Bernardino Historical Society, featuring an article: "Fred T. Perris: Pioneer and Energizer" by Larry E. Burgess

4) From the Gloucester Newspapers on microfilm of 1849 in the public library, Gloucester, England

5) *"In Pursuit of the Golden Dream Reminiscences of San Francisco and the Northern and Southern Mines, 1849-1857"* by Howard C. Gardiner, edited by Dale L. Morgan, Western Hemisphere Inc. Stoughton, Massachusetts, 1970 pg 33-44

6) Unpublished manuscript (one page biography of Fred T. Perris) by V.M Feltskig of San Gabriel, granddaughter of Fred T. Perris, located in the local history room of San Diego Public Library

7) *"Mama Describes her Grandmother, Fanny Jane Perris Jennings"* Erma Hicken, Nov. 14, 1971. (Unpublished manuscript in the possession of Verda Hicken, great granddaughter of Fanny Jane Perris, Logan, Utah.)

8) Personal recollections of Perris S. Jensen (father of the author) of the stories he was told of his grandmother, Fanny Jane Perris Jennings Wilson.

9) *"Southern Cross Saints, The Mormons in Australia"* pg 224 by Marjorie Newton, The Institute for Polynesian Studies, Laie, Hawaii 1991.

10) Mormonism Americanism and Politics, Richard Vetterli, p383-457 Ensign Publishing Co., Salt Lake City, Utah 1961

11) Captain Jefferson Hunt of the Mormon Battalion wrote to Brigham Young, May 14, 1847, from Los Angeles regarding Rancho Chino

> "We have a very good offer to purchase a large valley, sufficient to support 50,000 families, connected with other excellent country, which might be obtained. The ranch connected with the valley is 5 about thirty miles from this place, and about twenty miles from a good ship landing. We may have the land and stock consisting of eight thousand head of cattle, the increase of which were three thousand last year, and an immense quantity of horses, by paying 500 dollars down, and taking our own time to pay the remainder, if we had only the privilege to buy it. There are excellent water privileges on it." (Journal History of the Church, Church Historian's Office. Salt Lake City, Utah)

12) Heritage of the Valley San Bernardino's First Century pg, 171 by George William Beattie and Helen Pruitt Beattie, Biobooks, Oakland, Calif. 1951 (Feldheym *op. cit.*)

13) The Mormons in San Bernardino, pg. 9 by Arda M. Haenszel, San Bernardino County Museum Association, Redlands, California, 1992. also History of San Bernardino and Riverside Counties pg. 38. John Brown, Jr., and James Boyd, Western Historical Association (1922)

14) Haenszel, *op. cit.* (ref #13)

15) "The Mormons in California—1846-1857" pp 74-75 Flora Belle Houston, Master of Arts Thesis, Univ. of California, Berkeley 1929

16) Ingersoll's Century Annuls of San Bernardino County, 1769-1904, Luther A. Ingersoll, Los Angeles 1904 pg 131 (Feldheym Library;, San Bernardino)

17) Survey Notes of Fred Perris found in the Fred T. Perris envelope at the Bancroft Library, University of California, Berkeley

18) San Bernardino County Recorder's Office. August 24, 1854 Hannah purchased Lot 7 of Block 45, facing north on 7th Street, one lot west of Utah Street. Fred purchased Lot 4 in Block 46, facing west on Utah Street, one lot south of 7th Street.

19) "Biography of Fanny Jane Perris" author unknown *op. cit.* (ref Biography of Fanny Jane Perris" author unknown (Unpublished manuscript in the Hicken collection, *op. cit.*)

20) *www.ci.san-bernardino.ca.us/about/history/4th_of_july.asp*

21) San Bernardino, The Rise and Fall of a California Community, Edward Leo Lyman, Signature Books, 1996 pg 340

22) Bancroft's Works, Vol. 26, pgs 455-61

23) *"Orrin Porter Rockwell, Man of God, Son of Thunder"* by Harold Schindler, University of Utah Press, Salt Lake City, 1966

24) Beattie, pg 312, *op. cit.*

25) *"Great Basin Kingdom"*, Leonard J. Arrington pg 177 reprinted University of Utah Press, Salt Lake City, 1993

26) The Utah Mormons made no attempt to reestablish their organization in San Bernardino until 1922. A branch of the Reorganized Church of Jesus Christ of Latter Day Saints, headquartered in Independence, Missouri and which also holds Joseph Smith to be a prophet, had a branch in San Bernardino in the 19th century; but that should not be confused with the Utah group.

27) *"Fred Thomas Perris—1857 to 1874"* by Charles Lloyd Hornbeck, a descendant, 1984 (unpublished manuscript found in the Perris Family envelope of the Feldheym Library, California Room, San Bernardino, CA)

28) Excerpts from The Diary of Fred T. Perris, (in the possession of Mike Cowan, San Bernardino. great grandson of Fred T. Perris.)

29) Perris Jensen, *op. cit.* (ref. 8)

30) Hornbeck, *op. cit. (ref 27)*

31) "The Autobiography of James C. Jensen," unpublished manuscript by the nephew of Fred T. Perris.

32) According to Wikipedia a new photographic process was developed in 1851 by Frederick Scott Archer, a sculptor, by pouring collodion (nitrocellulose) on a glass plate, then dipping the plate into a solution of potassium iodide and silver nitrate such that it left a coat of silver iodide on the surface. This was exposed in the camera, and then developed in ferrous sulfate or oxalate (later pyrogallol) and fixed with sodium thiosulfate. To work away from a studio, the photographer had to have a portable dark-tent. This method was in use for about twenty years, and was used by Mathew Brady in the Civil War.

33) Fred's sister Emily, (who remained in Van Wert, Ohio while her mother was in England) received child support from the Thomas Perris estate in the amount of 40 British pounds per year, until her 21st birthday, at which time she got one third of £4,000, according to: Affidavit by Emily Augusta Perris of May 6, 1870 (Hicken collection *op. cit.*)

34) My notes of 17 years ago record that Mathew Stewart joined the Ohio Cavalry and was assigned to McLaughlin's 1st Squadron, Company B; but I have lost the reference source as to where that information was found.

35) "Hannah Rebecca Spiller" by Albert Zobell, Jr. *Improvement Era*, January 1952 (found as a mimeographed sheet in the Perris Family envelope of the Feldheym Library, California Room, San Bernardino, CA; also posted as an exhibit in the Perris Valley Historical Museum, Perris, CA

36) *The Evening Deseret News*, July 1862, in reporting on entries to the "State Fair" mentions Fred Perris, in the photography exhibit, showing his ambrotypes. The area was still a territory. The use of the term "State" refers to the State of Deseret. (LDS Church Historian's Office, Salt Lake City.)

The Evening Deseret News, January 1863, a reporter says the folks in Santaquin were amazed and amused when Brother Perris, using a strong magnifying glass and a lantern showed an audience his photographs. (LDS Church Historian's Office, Salt Lake City)

"Wayward Saints, the Godbeites and Brigham Young" by Ronald W. Walker, University of Illinois Press, Urbana, IL 1998 Pg 61 informs us that the firm, Ambrotype Gallery of Perris and Hopkins, had been located next door to the Telegraph Office.

37) *"History of Utah"* Vol.2, Orson F. Whitney, pp 48-57, George Q. Cannon, 1893 also see: http://www.wikipedia.org. Search for: Morrisite War.

38) *The Book of Mormon*, published by the LDS Church, Salt Lake City, Utah, the foundation document of the movement, is another witness of the Lord's dealings with His people, equal in doctrinal weight to The Bible. It identifies the American Indians as Lamanites, descendants of Israel through Laman, who left Jerusalem about 600 BCE, and sailed to America. His descendants were cursed with a "dark skin" for their disbelief in the god of their fathers, Abraham, Isaac and Jacob.

39) *"History of Idaho,"* Leonard J. Arrington, Vol. 1 pg 268 University of Idaho Press, Moscow, Idaho 1994

40) *"Bury My Heart at Wounded Knee"* by Dee Brown, pp 85-91 Holt, Rinehart &Winston, New York 1971

41) Arrington *"History of Idaho,"* Vol. 1, pg 271 cites the Minutes of the High Council Meeting, August 23, 1863 (found in the Brigham Young Collection of the LDS Church Library Archives, 176-80) also see: Bancroft's Works, Vol. XXVI History of Utah, 1540-1886, pg 631. The History Company Publishers, San Francisco, 1889

42) Arrington HI, pg 273, *op. cit.* (ref #40)

43) Encyclopedia Britannica, 1967 Vol. 10, pg 892

44)

    July 2, 1864

    Mr. Frederick T. Peris and others in Engineers Camp
    U.P.R.R Survey.
    Brethren:

    I have received your communication of June 29th and have duly considered your proposition, and in reply I wish to state that I cannot consistently entertain the idea of paying you your wages in gold. It is true that Greenbacks is (sic) at present at considerable discount, but not a great deal more so than when you were engaged, and of course your wages were based somewhat upon that consideration. There is nothing certain about the present discount, it may be but the panic of the hour. Be that as it may, my advice to you is to continue the work, and say nothing about gold or greenbacks at present, and when the work is completed, if the pay does not suit you, you can invest your money in shares in the company which will be better to you all, than either gold or greenbacks. This is all that I have opportunity to write upon the subject at present. Go on with the work that you have begun and all will work out right.

Your Brother in the Gospel.
Brigham Young

July 13, 1864

Brother Frederick Peris
and Brother Slaugh:

I am informed by Mr. Reed that a portion of the employees attached to the surveying party and in the field are dissatisfied about their wages, and threaten to quit, &c, &c Now I wish to say to all such that I consider their action in this matter the heighth (sic) of ingratitude, to say the very least of it. They originally came to me and offered their services, and I plainly told them what was required, and what wages I should pay, and they consented to go. We helped some here under wages some five or six weeks, doing nothing butting Mr. Reed's arrival. I am furnishing their families with flour at $6.00 per hundred when I could get at the rate of $10 to $12 in gold for it, and other provisions proportionably (sic) cheap, and now all I demand of them is that they shall fulfill their agreement and go on and finish the job like honorable men, and not try to take an advantage of me now because they think I cannot get another set of hands in season to carry on the work. They will probably all want work again. I would not like their course in this matter to be such as to debar them from the confidence and employ of good men.

I wish you to read this communication to all who are dissatisfied, and tell them to stop their grumbling and growling as I did not hire them to do that, but to attend to their work and to whatever is required of them in camp.

Your Brother in the Gospel
Brigham Young

45) Letter from Fred T. Perris to William S. Godbe, (ref #65) makes reference to their meeting in 1866 in New York and discussing their mutual concern for affairs in Utah.

46) The Salt Lake Directory, 1867

47) *"Documentary History of the Church"* lists a Deseret News article dated 1868, which praises Fred T. Perris, after his recent return from a successful buying trip for Cronyn and Perris, on West Temple Street. (LDS Church Historian's Office, Salt Lake City, Utah)

48) Hornbeck, *op. cit.* (ref #27)

49) "Nothing ever succeeds as planned" is Gold's Law, named for Bruce Gold, fictional hero of Joseph Heller's novel, "Good as Gold" It's a whole book about getting what you want, as opposed to wanting what you get.

Creators of art and other objects point to their works and say, what you see is what they intended, in order to make a sale; but creative people are often driven by an attempt to make something better than the previous version of whatever it is they are trying to create. Original intent is continuously updated, and thus meaningless.

50) Wealthy Mormons attribute their prosperity to the promise made by Malachi, the last prophet of the Old Testament Chapter 3, verse 10:

> "Bring ye all the tithes into the storehouse, that there may be meat in mine house, and prove me now herewith, saith the Lord of hosts, if I will not open you the windows of heaven and pour you out a blessing, that there shall not be room enough to receive it."

A tithing contribution paid to the Church is considered a wise business investment.

51) Arrington "Great Basin Kingdom" pg 248 (ref #25)

52) Bancroft *op. cit.* pg 654 (ref #40)

53) *"The Rocky Mountain Saints,"* pp 629-34, Thomas Brown Holmes Stenhouse, (1825-1882) D. Appleton and Company, New York, 1873 (found in U. of U. Library, Level 4, call BX8611.S76)

54) Stenhouse, *op. cit.* pg 639 (ref #52)

55) Bancroft, *op. cit.* pg 649 (ref #40)

56) Stenhouse, *op. cit.* pg 639 (ref #52)

57) Bancroft Vol. XXVI (HU) pg 649 (ref 40)

58) *The Deseret Evening News*, Oct. 26, 1869 (Microfilm copy in the Marriott Library, University of Utah, Salt Lake City, Utah)

59) The LDS Church has made dramatic changes in its turbulent history, notably when it renounced the practice of polygamy in 1890, and when it changed its racial policy in 1978 and ordained men of African descent to the Priesthood. In both cases the change was announced by the living Prophet; and, it is claimed, in the former case had nothing to do with the fact that Congress would not admit Utah into the Union until they gave up polygamy, nor in the latter case that the Church was threatened with losing its tax exempt status if it continued its practice of racial discrimination. Mormons adamantly refuse to believe these outside pressures had any effect upon Church policy.

It was only when God spoke through His Prophet that the changes were instituted. Likewise, Mormons refused then, and now, to acknowledge the many smaller changes that came about coincident with pressure from *The Salt Lake Tribune*.

60) Documentary History of the Church, *op. cit.* Letter from George Q. Cannon (ref #47)

61) Tullidge's Histories, pg 306-12 (Marriott Library, University of Utah, Salt Lake City)

62) Perris Jensen *op. cit.* (ref #8)

63) Microfilm copies of virtually all issues of The Salt Lake Tribune are found in the Marriott Library, University of Utah, Salt Lake City. Notably absent are the issues when the entire text of the secret temple ceremony and rites were published in the newspaper.

64) "Orrin Porter Rockwell, *Man of God, Son of Thunder*", pp 44-48, Harold Schindler, University of Utah Press, Salt Lake City, Utah 1966.

65) Letter from Fred T. Perris to William S. Godbe found in the Hampton C. Godbe Collection, MS 664, Manuscripts Division, Special Collections, Marriott Library, University of Utah, Salt Lake City, Utah.)

San Bernardino, Cal
August 16, 1877

My dear friend William:

How can I sufficiently express my thanks and joy for your letter of the 6th inst? Words fail me and tears have been forced from the intensity of my emotion.

To feel and know that you fully and thoroughly understand the situation and that I am not compromised in your, and other friends estimation is a relief to me you can here only estimate. I am also greatly assured to hear of your very high opinion of Mr. Howard as this relieves me also of much embarrassment. Judging from the attack made on him by both the Herald & Tribune, he is the right man in the right place and will yet accomplish much if not goaded too far by the radicals.

Within a day or two after the receipt of yours, came words of consolation and cheer from William & E. L. T. which I do assure you, and them, are highly treasured. Say to them I +will reply as quickly as possible. Now I want to make as full and complete a statement as possible, so that you may understand everything fully, and have enclosed original papers (Minutes of meetings for safe keeping to show you certain connections.)

It seems that I am believed to know all about the murders of John Banks, through being on guard with Serrine. Now this is not true. Were it otherwise I should feel myself at perfect liberty to tell all as I have never been under any obligation in relation to it, for it occurred prior to my connection with the police, and before I was thought to be trusted.

This should be proof enough that I have no desire to withhold anything pertaining to that brutal affair. The facts are these: It is well known that I was one of the guard at the time of the Morrisite affair; a private only. I then conscientiously believed I was doing my duty as one of a sheriff's posse, and stood up to it "like an Englishman," being made a target of a number of times, as I was afterward informed by a Morrisite. I mention this to show you that this had much to do with my being afterward called to take charge of the 7th Ward Police. At the close of the fight, when all was excitement, it was rumored among our men, that Morris and others had been shot in the endeavor to regain possession of their guns after the surrender, and that Banks had been seriously shot in the back of the neck. All this occurred as nearly as I can remember about 1/2 mile of where we were posted with our guard. This rumor was believed by our men and I presume Hopkins can corroborate my statement as we were together at the same post all day. I have no recollection of being on guard in the evening, as stated, still may have been. I do, however, remember distinctly seeing Banks, late in the evening, seated in a wagon smoking a pipe. This, in view of the rumor, created in me great surprise as it was announced that he was badly or seriously wounded. What took place after this I never knew. In the morning the announcement was made that Banks had died during the night. That he had died from the effects of his wound. I did not believe, having seen him smoking as above stated

My conclusion then was, and I have believed it until the receipt of your letter; that he had been poisoned during the night, but of course, I dared not express myself to that effect. The statement made that he was brutally murdered by an instrument from Dr. Taits case is as new to me as it can possibly be to anyone else. This is the extent of my knowledge in the Banks case.

The statements in regard to the secret organization, the oath, secretary ship are all true. You will see from original papers enclosed the invidious way in which it sprang into existence, first as meetings of the Captains of Special police, offered with "prayer" and closed by "benedictions." You will also see when and how I was first chosen Clerk, and of course why I was continued as such afterward in the closer organization. The object of that association is correctly stated, or at least that was it when first organized. It was but a similar arrangement to one effected in San Bernardino for self protection, shortly after the Mountain Meadow Massacre, and of which I believe Serrine was a member. The penalty, like that of the Endowment, was death to those who betrayed any of its passwords, secrets &c. This will enable you to understand why I had to act with so much caution after the inauguration of the "Movement," and how it served us so well for protection. Many of the outrages, prior to the assassination of Dr. R. doubtless sprang from the organization, but about that time you will remember that we, Cronyn & Co. or rather George Cronyn were receiving goods freighted by yourself & Mitchell across the plains, and which I had purchased the summer of 1866, that being my first trip East to purchase goods. Fred Auerbach, then our next door neighbor, will doubtless remember some of these circumstances. The intense amount of work at the store and in the office about that time caused me to be absent

48

from several meetings. Consequently I did not learn as much as I might otherwise have done. If I remember rightly this was also the year you and I had had a talk over Utah affairs in New York when we expressed mutual dissatisfaction.

About the time, or shortly after, a man connected with the Videtto had received a whipping on the street. Clinton proposed that Dr. R. should be whipped too with a view to scaring him out of this endeavor to squat on land near Warm Springs. I was at the meeting and never thought for a moment of anything more serious growing out of it. You may judge of my horror, when a day or two afterward on coming up into Town to the Store I heard of the brutal murder committed the night before. It was only then that the whole force of the great danger I had been in, and the fearful consequences of ever formalizing a clue to the perpetration burst upon me. As time had elapsed between the proposed whipping and the committal of the crime, I never positively knew who were the actual participants, nor whether they received private instructions, to do as they did, or whether the exigency arose through an attempt of Dr. R. to defend himself. I already knew more than I wanted too, and did not ask a question for I did not want to learn more.

Following are other facts you are familiar with as they relate to the opening of the Movement.

I cannot see any other honorable course left me but to assist Mr. H. to the extent of my power, notwithstanding the consequences are such that I can not contemplate them. I have here, regained the esteem and respect of the people, who have honored me with two positions of Trust, County Surveyor & Town Engineer. To become a witness under the circumstances, will blight my whole future here and measurably ostracize me from society, for you will know that strangers cannot and will not view matters from your storefront and that of my friends. This contingency and its effect upon my family appals [sic] me, more than the possibility of assassination to get me out of the way. I rely wholly upon your friendship and the consideration of Mr. H. to sustain me in the future.

To have yourself and Mr. Howard drop down on a visit here would be most gratifying. Still I can (?) (?) that you can take time to get away from business.

Let me hear from you on receipt of this and Believe me.

Faithfully yours
Fred T. Perris.

Since penning the enclosed I have received a note from Mr. Howard asking for a full statement in the Bank matter and have referred him to you. I cannot understand why or how it is thought I know so much about it, unless somebody is guessing that I ought to know on general principles.

I cannot possibly say more than I have already as it comprises everything I remember. Were this otherwise I would gladly say so for the reasons already set forth. What was done with Bank or how it was done I have never known until your letter reached me, and I am greatly surprised to find that "I must have seen and heard enough to convince me of the murder." You must bear in mind that at the time Serrine had charge of the Brass gun and that I was but a "private" at another's game, and that therefore he may have learned more than I did, through his closer connection. Now I want to plead with you to use your influence with Mr. H. to keep me out of the witness box if possible. If enough evidence exists this can be done. I do not want the awful stigma necessarily following to attach to my family. You can thoroughly realize my feeling in this regard being in possession of the facts.

I care not for myself but the prospect so far as my family is concerned fills me with anguish.

Let me hear from you immediately,

Faithfully yours,
Fred

66) The Diary of Hans Hoth, pg 135 Unpublished manuscript in the Bancroft Library, University of California, Berkeley.

67) Zobell, *op. cit.* (ref #9)

68) Burgess, *op. cit.* (ref #3)

69) Weekly Journal of Thomas Jefferson Evans 1863-1901. Unpublished manuscript in the Perris Museum.

ABOUT THE AUTHOR

Neil Jensen grew up in a house full of books, forever curious about their content. Yet, despite the reverence, almost awe, that he acquired from his bibliomaniac father, for scholarship, for having the wisdom of the ages on a bookshelf nearby, Neil did not pursue a scholarly career. Rather he got a degree in engineering, and spent 15 years in hard labor, doing penance for that misdeed, compelled to build rockets, and nose cones for missiles, and nuclear fuel for fun and corporate profits.

Then, one day came that ah-ha moment in the turmoil of a mid-life crisis, when he realized that engineers do all that they do with only ten numbers, arranged in a variety of ways; whereas there are twenty six letters, meaning that there must be at least 2.6 times more ways to combine letters than numbers, maybe more. And from that day on, his interests turned to the theatre, the written word, and the spoken word.

He served, for a period of 20 years, on the board of the Playwrights' Center of San Francisco, a non-profit which produced, during that time, more than 1,000 concert-staged readings of original plays. It was inevitable that he would eventually return to the passion of his youth, historical research.

He set out, one day, to find the famous Uncle Fred, his great grandmother's brother, who, his father said, had two towns in the country named after him. This book is the result of that search.

He still lives in the Silicon Valley with a house full of books, a patient wife, and an overbearing cat.